Women Empowerment and Sustainable Development

Women Empowerment and Sustainable Development

Dr. Anupama Singh

Institute of Integrated Himalayan Studies
H.P. University, Shimla
in association with
KANISHKA PUBLISHERS, DISTRIBUTORS
NEW DELHI-110 002

KANISHKA PUBLISHERS, DISTRIBUTORS
4697/5-21 A, Ansari Road, Daryaganj
New Delhi-110 002
Phones : 2327 0497, 2328 8285
Fax : 011-2328 8285
E-mail: kanishka_publishing@yahoo.co.in

First Published 2008

ISBN 978-81-8457-019-9

PRINTED IN INDIA

Published by Madan Sachdeva for Kanishka Publishers, Distributors, 4697/5-21A, Ansari Road, Daryaganj, New Delhi-110 002, Typeset by Sunshine Graphics, Delhi, and Printed at Nice Printing Press, Delhi.

Acknowledgements

Professor L.R. Verma, Ex-Vice-Chancellor, HP University for his encouragement and cooperation towards this study.

Professor Yoginder Verma, Director, Institute of Integrated Himalayan Studies, for his support and constructive guidance to bring this research to conclusion.

All the teachers of Himachal Pradesh University who were directly or indirectly associated with the study, whose continuous stimulation of intellectual atmosphere honed my understanding of the issue.

The State Resource Centre, Shimla (HP) for its help rendered during the data collection, a number of activists for their commitment to the rural people of Himachal Pradesh.

Authors, writers of various books articles, reports for their insights, understanding, perception and their work which I consulted and cited at various places.

All the respondents "Rural Women, Government, a number of NGOs active in Shimla for narrating their experiences and providing required information.

Gopal Krishan Narwal and Sanjay Angra, Computer Experts for typing and programming the work.

Dr. Anupama Singh

Preface

In most of the mountain communities women play a major role in farming activities and in exploitation of common property resources. It is observed that women's participation in conservation and sustaining development initiatives is most often affected by their minimum decision-making power in household, the farm and the community. Women's empowerment and mainstreaming of gender concerns are thus essential and indispensable for any sustainable development action. Women empowerment is also critical to succeed in the development tasks that face many nations. The contributions of women are as much necessary as those of men. Social, economic and political rights are inseparable in practice and entwined for a collective and community development.

Development must be gender sensitive if it is to be equitable, sustainable and effective. Participation and community engagements are important determinants of sustainable development, a concept which addresses issues of social equity and political legitimacy and not merely the efficient provision of infrastructure and public services. The various ways in which women and men participate in and benefit from development activities are significantly shaped by prevailing construction of gender, norms, practices, expectations and institutional procedures constrain women's access to the social and economic and thus political resources of a community. Generally societies attribute roles and responsibilities to women and men differently but fail to value or even account the crucial contributions women's labour makes to household and community maintenance. Paradoxically, such social reproduction allows little or no time for women to part take in activities, which might help them to determine their own lives.

Full development may not be achieved unless women and the resources they represent are fully integrated into the development. Expansion in gender equality and women's empowerment is vital for improving economic, social and political conditions in communities within the framework of sustainable development.

This study recognizes that the adoption of women empowerment as an objective for sustainable, people-centered development implies a more comprehensive approach than previously followed development approaches. This research explores two primary areas women empowerment as a tool to sustain the development as an ongoing process. In the first chapter the concepts of Women Empowerment and Sustainable Development are discussed. An attempt has been made to trace the evolution of both the concepts and their meaning to people even at the local level. The focus of the study is women empowerment and how this issue is encountered in their lives as an agents of change and development. It is recognized that there is no acknowledgement of their contribution to agriculture and household services. In the second chapter the socio-economic profile of the rural women is examined. It is appraised that the socio-economic status defines the levels of interaction with the rest of the environment in the society. In this part of the study many variables i.e., age, caste, education, occupation, property, family are evaluated. Chapter III provides some insights into the social norms of the hill society and its impact on the lives of women. Chapter IV concretely demonstrates implications of political empowerment amongst women. It tries to illustrate that a focus on political empowerment is essential to the achievements of other development objectives as well as important in its own right. Chapter V discusses how of women is dependent on the outside agencies i.e., non-governmental agencies and government agencies capacities to incorporate gender equality concerns in social, economic and political development concerns. It reiterates the fact that there is sufficient scope and capacity for women's empowerment to mainstream development partnership. In Chapter VI the role of environment in the lives of rural women is discussed. It explores how the daily chores of rural women so closely associated and influenced by the immediate environment. In the last Chapter, it is concluded that despite an obvious presence as citizens, women stay under-represented in governing structures. With only a few exceptions, there is a marked absence of women in local decision-making processes. Although women are key players at the local level in household livelihood strategies and residential organizations, they are generally excluded from important decision-making forums. Even where due to reservation of 33 per cent for women in local bodies is imminent, women do not yet feel prepared enough to take decisions, due to which the concept of Pati Panchayats has surfaced i.e., proxy rule by husbands. It would be befitting to add that references made in Item 9 of IULA World Wide Declaration on Women in local government, 1998: The problem and the challenges facing humanity are global but have to be dealt with at the local level. Women have the equal right to freedom from poverty, discrimination, environment degradation and insecurity. To fight these problems and to meet the challenges of sustainable development, it is crucial that women be empowered and involved in local government as decision-makers, planners and managers.

Dr. Anupama Singh

Contents

List of Abbreviations

AMC	Advanced Measurement Approach
ARC	Agricultural Refinance Corporation
ARCs	Asset Reconstruction Companies
ARF	Asset Reconstruction Fund
AS	Available for Sale
BCBS	Basel Committee on Banking Supervision
BFS	Board for Financial Supervision
BIA	Basic Indicator Approach
BIFR	Board for Industrial and Financial Reconstruction
BIS	Bank for International Settlement
BPLR	Benchmark Prime Lending Rate
BSE	Bombay Stock Exchange
CAR	Capital Adequacy Ratio
CBI	Central Bureau of Investigation
CBS	Core Banking Solutions
CCF	Credit Conversion Factor
CDR	Corporate Debt Restructuring Mechanism
CFC	Customer Facilitation Centre
CFS	Committee on Financial System
CMD	Chief Managing Director
CPWG	Core Principles Working Group
CRR	Cash Reserve Ratio
CTS	Cheque Truncation System
DCA	Debtor-Creditor Agreement
DICGC	Deposit Insurance and Credit Guarantee Corporation
DIR	Differential Interest Rates

DRTs	Debt Recovery Tribunals
DSCR	Debt Service Coverage Ratio
EAD	Exposure at Default
EB	Efficiency Bar
ECGC	Export Credit Guarantee Corporation
ECS	Electronic Clearing System
FBs	Foreign Banks
FIs	Financial Institutions
FRA	Forward Rate Agreement
FRMS	Fraud Reporting and Monitoring System
GOI	Government of India
HT	Held for Trading
HTM	Held to Maturity
IAS	Indian Accounting Standards
IBA	Indian Banks Association
ICA	Inter-Creditor Agreement
IDRBT	Institute for Development and Research in Banking Technology
IFR	Investment Fluctuation Reserve
IRS	Interest Rate Swaps
KCC	Kisan Credit Card
KYCs	Know Your Customers
LGD	Loss Given Default
LIE	Least Interested Employees
MICR	Magnetic Character Ink Recognition
MPBF	Maximum Permissible Bank Finance
MRC	Minimum Regulatory Capital
NABARD	National Bank for Agricultural and Rural Development
NDTLs	Net Demand and Time Liabilities
NEFT	National Electronic Funds Transfer
NEWBK	New Bank of India
NGOs	Non-Government Organizations
NII	Net Interest Income

NPAs	Non-Performing Assets
NSE	National Stock Exchange
PD	Probability of Default
PLR	Prime Lending Rate
PNB	Punjab National Bank
PSBs	Public Sector Banks
PSIBs	Private Sector Indian Banks
PSUs	Public Sector Undertakings
RBI	Reserve Bank of India
RCs	Reconstruction Companies
RIDF	Rural Infrastructure Development Fund
RRBs	Regional Rural Banks
RTGS	Real Time Gross Settlements
RWA	Risk Weighted Assets
SA	Standardized Approach
SARF-ARESI	Securitisation and Reconstruction of Financial Assets and Enforcement of Security Interest
SCs	Securitisation Companies
SEFT	Special Electronic Funds Transfer
SHGs	Self-Help Groups
SHPIs	Self-Help Promoting Institutions
SIDBI	Small Industries Development Bank of India
SIPS	Systematically Important Payment System
SLR	Statutory Liquidity Ratio
STP	Straight Through Processing
VRS	Voluntary Retirement Scheme
YTM	Yield to Maturity

1

Women Empowerment and Sustainable Development in Himachal Pradesh

This study aims to contribute in highlighting some of the concepts of women empowerment, equality and its impact on sustainable development. The focus of this study is basically to research the level of awareness of social, political, economic and environmental issues amongst rural women in Himachal Pradesh. These conclusions will also lead to certain parameters, whether more empowered women would be instrumental in sustainable development.

Hence, *key words* – Women Empowerment, Sustainable Development.

The objective is to concentrate on the issues of women, which have been dealt with either by the voluntary agencies or governmental agencies or simultaneously by both or have not been dealt so far. It is seen that traditional gender gap have been re-endorsed in the new development paradigms where unequal access to resources or outcome of resources has been established. It is an effort at covering these vast and interconnected issues. The study begins with a review of definitions and conceptual issues of women empowerment.

Conceptualizing Women Empowerment

Women have been interacting with the environment since the ages. But only since the nineties the role of women as the key players in sustainable development has been established. The UN Millennium Development Goals[1] suggests that having an equal voice in the decisions that affect their lives from within the family to the loftiest realms of government—is a key element of women empowerment where gender equality should be treated as a human right which certainly means equality at all levels of education and in all areas equal control over resources and equal representation in public and political life.

It is a fact that rural poor are immediately affected because their day-to-day subsistence and livelihoods more often depend on the natural resources around them. For rural women too, it means empowerment in several aspects personal, familial, economic and political. It seems that everywhere economic and political power appear to be equally necessary components of empowerment.

Taking account of Gita Sen's definition of empowerment as the process by which powerless gain greater control over the circumstances of their lives, the working group considered empowerment to focus on individual women, as well as women collectively. Good governance predicated respect for human rights, transparency, and access to knowledge, resources and decision-making as well as participation, all of which were essential for empowerment.[2]

Women empowerment can be defined as a condition in which women hold or are in the process of obtaining educational, legal and political rights that are equivalent or nearly equal to those of male citizens. Empowerment extends beyond the acts or attitude of government, for it should also include women's increased knowledge of the history of women in their own country/region, and social and psychological effects of patriarchy.

Access and control over certain resources makes some groups gain control over others in the society—the focus on the control over material resources, productive resources and human resources is clear. The control over intellectual resources, such as knowledge and information and also the capacity to have ideas and think in new ways gives a great deal of power.[3] We may find many changes in the concept of women empowerment, but studies since 1970s emphasize the importance of the phenomena of 'power to'—that is certainly power to bring about changes in situations of inequity and discrimination in which women find themselves. Since 1970s, the meaning of women empowerment has certainly expanded which has made it a process rather than an outcome. So, at different places women may be at different stages of empowerment. The objective may be equity and parity in access to resources and decision-making which influence their lives rather than a single goal.

We may be able to define women empowerment as the definition used in the United Nations. It includes—women's sense of self worth; their right to have and determine choices; their right to have the power to control their own lives, both within and outside home; and their ability to influence the direction of social change to create a more just social and economic order nationally and internationally.

However, in this context women empowerment certainly addresses the issue of power relations. It occurs when women empowerment addresses issues, which marginalize women in the process of development, and the very agencies are asked to change their approach in policy making and take decisions, which are gender sensitive. When we talk about empowerment of women it does not necessarily mean the disempowerment of men, of their rights and privileges which patriarchy gave them. Though it does help men who have long been sitting unquestionably in the seats of decision-making to become more gender sensitive and to have a more equal work.

Women empowerment certainly also means the recognition of women and their contribution to development process. The seminar[4] in Stockholm revealed "the complexity of defining empowerment and the need to view it as incorporating many dimensions and facts. There was general agreement that empowerment is about transfor-mation of power relations; that it includes both control over material resources, and a change in self-perception and confidence in ones self; that it can be viewed both as an outcome and a process; and that women's empowerment of power relations at four different levels; the household/family, the community, the markets and the state."

For Batliwala[5] women's empowerment is thus the process, and the outcome of the process, by which women gain greater control over material and intellectual resources, and challenge the ideology of patriarchy and the gender-based discrimination against women in all the institutions and structures of society.

UN Population Information Network define women empowerment as:

> "Women empowerment has five components: Women's sense of self-worth, their right to have and to determine choices; their right to have access to opportunities and resources; their right to have the power to control their own lives, both within and outside the home, and their ability to influence the direction of social change to create a more just, social and economic order, nationally and internationally."

Basically, women's empowerment is the process (and its outcomes) in which women-individually and collectively—become active, knowledgeable and goal oriented actors who take/or support initiatives to overcoming gender inequalities. Hence, women's empowerment refers to a strategy to achieve gender equality as well as to the inherent capacity building processes.[6]

For Information for Development Glossary (IDG) empowerment corresponds to women challenging existing power structure, which subordinate women. As such, what is seen as empowering in one context may not be in another. Empowerment is not about reversing existing power hierarchies but rather about empowering women and/or women's groups to make their own choices, to speak out on their own behalf and control their own lives.

The concept of women empowerment of an individual or a social group pre-supposes that a state of social oppression exists which has dis-empowered those in the groups, by denying them opportunities or resources and by subjecting them to an ideology and a set of social practices which has defined them as inferior humans, thus lowering their self-esteem.

It is important to know women empowerment to allow us to know as we see it in people with whom we are working for the project evaluation. How we choose to define empowerment depends upon the specific women and context involved. Generally, empowerment may be a multi-dimensional social process that helps people gain control over their own lives.

Page and Czuba[7] (1999) suggest three components of our definition to understanding women empowerment: it is multidimensional, social and a process. It is multi-dimensional in the sense that it occurs within sociological, psychological, economic and other dimensions, empowerment also occurs at various levels, such as individual, group and community. Empowerment by definition is a social process, since it occurs in relationship to others. Empowerment is a process that is similar to a path journey, one that develops as we work through it. Other aspects of empowerment may vary according to the specific context and people involved but these remain constant. In addition, one important implication of this definition of empowerment is that the individual and community are fundamentally connected.

The national as well as international community has recognized the empowerment of women as a vital element in national development. This is equally true in building a society based on equality and equanimity where wide disparities exist within a county amongst its people, through various cross-sections of the society. So it is equally important that developments that shape tomorrows' society should and must persue the goals of gender equality and women's advancement, as well as social, political and economic justice, and sustainable human development.

The focus of this study is not only women empowerment but also how this issue is encountered in the lives of rural women. Rural women combat oppression at generally two levels i.e. by their class and gender. They experience marginalization not only in terms of resources but also have no or minimal access to information and services. They are invisible in the government surveys of rural areas, and if reported, they are represented as mere receivers rather than having any active role in development. There is almost no recognition of their contribution to agriculture and household services, but rarely receive measurable economic gains from government programmes. Empowering of rural women must be pursued vigorously not only for the reason that they are active players in all agricultural activities but also for the fact they are extremely marginalized which gravely contradicts with their right as a human being. It is important that they participate in all spheres of decision-making, which have long or short-term influence on their lives.

Within the framework of a democratic polity, Indian laws, development policies, plans and programme have aimed at women's advancement in different spheres from the mid-seventies (1974-78). During the Fifth Five-Year Plan onwards, there has been a marked shift in the approach to women's issues from welfare to development. In recent years, the empowerment of women has been recognized as the central issue in determining the status of women. The National Commission for Women was set-up by an act of parliament on 1990 to safeguard the rights and legal entitlements of women. The 73rd and 74th Amendments of the Constitution of India (1993) have provided for reservation of seats in the local bodies of Panchayats and Municipalities for women, laying a strong foundation for their participation in decision-making at the local levels. In a quiet revolution, nearly a million women now occupy positions as members and chairpersons of local bodies.[8]

India has also ratified various international conventions and human rights instruments committing to secure equal rights to women. Key among them is the ratification of the Convention on Elimination of all forms of Discrimination Against Women (CEDAW) in 1993. The Mexico Plan of Action (1975), the Nairobi Forward Looking Strategies (1985), the Beijing Declaration (1995) as well as the Platform for Action (1995) and the outcome Document adopted by UNGA session on Gender Equality and Development and Peace for the 21st century, titled "Further Actions and Initiatives to Implement the Beijing Declaration and the Platform for Action" have been unreservedly endorsed by India for appropriate follow-up. The policy also takes note of the commitments of the Ninth Five Year Plan and sectoral policies five-year plans and sectoral policies relating to empowerment of women.

However, there still exists a wide gap between the goals enunciated in the constitution, legislation, policies, plans, programme[9] and related mechanisms on the one hand and situational reality of the status of women in India.

Bannerjee (1998)[10] finds out that report of Towards Equality (1974) that "Indian statue had failed in its constitutional obligation of not discriminating on the grounds of gender." The review of the disabilities and constraints on women, which stem from socio-cultural institutions, indicates that the majority of women are still—very far from enjoying the rights and opportunities guaranteed to them by the constitution. The social laws, that sought to mitigate the problems of women in their family life, have remained unknown to a large mass of women in this country, who are ignorant of their legal rights today as they were before independence (Towards Equality, 1974, 359). Once again various movement raised concerned voices regarding the position and rights of women in Indian society.

Rajan[11] finds that the Commissions appointed by the Government of India to review the status of women from time-to-time, along with action plans, culminating in 1998 in the adoption of the National Perspective Plan for Woman, have carried out several in-depth studies. This plan, based on the position of women and the constraints they face, charts out the action required of the Central (Union) and the State Government in particular, and all others concerned in general. In a detailed manner the plan concentrates on rural women and stresses that policy must aim at bringing women into the mainstream of the national economy.

Rajan (1995) recognizes that without empowerment of women, especially in the decision-making process at the lower levels, most of what we wish to achieve will not be easy. A statutory National Commission for Women has broad mandate and the authority to overall measures and to recommend to India State Government what further course of action needs to be initiated in different areas. He emphasizes the role of NGOs and the kind of interactions that should exist between Government and NGO's in promoting women's development. Perhaps at this stage

Government action may be essential to complement and supplement the NGOs working to end isolation of women from the mainstream national economy and assist them to play the role due to them through training and the removal of socio-cultural-economic barriers.

National Policy of Empowerment, 2001[12] clearly illustrates its objectives:

(*a*) To bring about advancement, development and empowerment of women.
(*b*) To eliminate all forms of discrimination against women.
(*c*) To ensure active participation of women in all spheres of life.

Themes and issues concerned in policy:

(*a*) Judicial legal system.
(*b*) Economic empowerment.
(*c*) Social empowerment including health, education, violence, science and technology, drinking water and sanitation.
(*d*) Women and decision-making, media and girl child etc.

It was felt as a basic need to translate the goals of international and national women agencies working for their welfare to translate these goals into actions at local levels. These goals had to be implemented on the women who had heard nothing of these organizations but could benefit from their outcome. So, for the first time, State level goals have been set for each state in addition to National targets. The women's component plan[13] which records the funds earmarked for schemes targeted to women and girls and those with a significant women's component is an effective mechanism in the planning process for targeting expenditure in favour of women.

Since India embarked upon a re-structuring of its economic policy framework in 1991, Globalization and structure adjustment have had varying sectoral impacts. Women have gained employment in new avenues, for example in information technology. These are mainly urban and educated women. However, an adverse impact on women's livelihood has been reported from different parts of the country, such as agriculture.[14] The report of National Commission on labour noted that with up gradation of skill, opportunities for employment of women exist in several areas such as health services, food processing and crafts.

Women and Poverty

Initiative taken by the Central Government to tackle poverty for women include the following:

- Providing women with access to saving and credit mechanism and institution through micro credit schemes.
- Skill and capacity building initiatives have gathered momentum in the recent years. The Self-Help Groups movement has been supported through schemes of a large number of departments including the women and child development, Rural Development, Handlooms and Handicrafts, Sericulture, Agriculture etc.
- Skill and capacity building interventions are supported through programmes such as:

    1. STEP (Support to Training and Employment Programme).
    2. Swawlamban, to train women for employment in traditional and non-traditional trades.
    3. Swashakti, a rural women's development empowerment project, Swaymasidha launched in 2001, the Integrated Women's Empowerment Programme, aimed at all round empowerment of women by ensuring their direct- access to and control over resources through sustained process

of mobilization and convergence of all on going sectoral programme.

4. For greater efficiency and better implementation, convergence of programme has been affected. All self-employment schemes for rural areas have been integrated into Swarnjayanti Gram Swarojgar Yojana launched in 1999. Forty per cent of the benefits are earmarked for women.
5. Anti-Poverty programmes have special focus on women. Thirty per cent of the employment oppor-tunities created under the wage employment scheme of Sampoorna Grameen Rojgar Yojana are reserved for women. The Indira Awas Yojana stipulates that houses under the schemes are to be allotted in the name of the female member of the beneficiary household.
6. Food security is ensured to poorest of the poor women through the Targeted Public Distribution System introduced in 1997.

Apart from this there are schemes and programmes for education, training, health, violence against women, human rights of women etc. Since our respondents are women in rural areas it will be worthwhile to see the reach of these programmes in the rural areas of Shimla.

Women and Environment

Women have traditionally been responsible for subsistence and survival tasks like providing water and food, fuel and fodder collection. The quality of rural environment directly affects women's livelihood. The nodal agency for activities relating to environment is the Ministry of Environment and Forests. Gender sensitive resource management is encouraging through several schemes including:

- The Joint Forest Management Schemes under which 50 per cent of the members are required to be women.

- Women's participation is encouraged in community resources management and watershed programme.
- Rural women living below the poverty line are provided with financial assistance to raise nurseries in forestlands.
- The Ministry of Non-Conventional Energy Sources is implementing several programmes to benefit women by reducing drudgery and providing better and convenient systems for cooking and highlighting.
- New initiatives to improve urban environment, especially water and sanitation, emphasize partnership between private community and government agencies.[15]

The point of mention in these policy initiatives by the Government of India is to see whether they have affected the livelihoods of women within the study region.

Introduction

The understating of development in terms of social, economic and political perspectives has changed tremendously in recent years. This draws the attention to the fact that environment has remained an integral part of any kind of development. The assessments of the role of environment and effects of development on it have become manifold with the rapid pace of development. The history of human development goes along with the history of climate and environment. The environment is the main factor in determining the growth and stability of civilizations. The human influence over the environment and climate now seem to consolidate a major problem because it is no longer a one way effect but now it has become a two way effect i.e., environment has begun to hit back at the civilization.

This analysis has brought the environment and climate as a factor to centre stage in all developmental and welfare policies. There is strong need to analyze the factors in the haze of development viz-a-viz climate as well as environment and their potential alternatives.

The industrial era started off with the Industrial Revolution in Britain in early 19th century. The limitation, depletion and conservation of natural resources was felt by many scholars of that era. The evidence of it can also be found in the literature and poetry of those times. Karl Marx perceived the problem of unsustainable development as consequence of the class structure of the society. The sustainability of food supplies and the loss of social fertility and land holdings were viewed as to reduce the food supplies in relation to future demand of the food.

The human exploitation of the earth's resources during the 20th century increased magnanimously especially due to rapid industrialization, deforestation and urbanization. The main component of environment exploitation biosphere is atmosphere, land cover and biodiversity. After the World War II, there was impending need to rebuild societies and bring about higher economic growth. This led to resource exploitation without paying attention to the indiscriminate methods, which ultimately almost endangered the human survival, flora and fauna, extinction of thousands of species, and irreversible damage to environment, which also managed to create a hole in the ozone layer.

In 1962, a book came out by Rachel Carson, Silent Springs, which is considered to be the first milestone for the modern environmental awareness and its social implications in developed countries. Her book dealt with the risks posed by a kind of pesticide i.e., dichlorodiphenyl trichloroethane (DDJ), which led to the extinction of many bird species. She examined life and sought "accommodation between humans and nature." Thomas Malthus, an economist was first to point out about the possibility of resources shortage due to their over exploitation with the incessant increase in population. The same views were again echoed with the release of "Limits to Growth" report by a group of countries, which called themselves "Club of Rome"(Meadows, *et.al.*, 1971). They made a computer projection of five components, which would help, define whether there actually existed anything like the limits to growth of earth's resources. These variables were: population, food, industrialization, non-renewable resources and pollution.

Interventions by the Institutions

The importance of environmental resource management took the global stage at the Stockholm conference on the Human Environment in 1972. Thousands of regional, national and international activities steered towards the idea of environmental preservation.

The policies, which were made in India after studying the constitutional provisions, would follow in the ensuing paragraphs. The need for commonality and interdependence of environmental issues led across to international boundaries to make certain international agreements that in fact laid the foundations for some very important global environmental actions. In this series United Nations on Human Environment held first conference at the world level on Swedish initiative. It also provided for permanent basis for international environment co-ordination and cooperation at the diplomatic front.

If 1972 onwards to 2000 is assumed as the first phase, Sustainable Development (SD) found its way into the environment related issues literature especially of the International Union for Conservation of Nature and Natural Resources (IUCN) around, 1980. A serious thought-provoking place was provided to the concept of sustainable development in the Brundtland Report on the world commission on environment and development. The report was published in 1987, with Gro Harlem Brundtland as the chairman.

A resolution of the United Nation's General Assembly in 1989 lead to the unprecedented UN Conference on Environment and Development (UNCED) popularly known as the Earth Summit held at Rio de Janeiro in June 1992. The summit was able to garner support of 118 nations. The Prime Minister of Norway, Gro Harlem Brundtland as "Progress in many fields, too little progress in most fields and no progress at all in some fields", summed up the result of the summit. It was popularly known as "Rio Declaration" setting forth 27 principles for sustainable development and an action plan known as "Agenda 21". The Sustainable Development approach emerged from the summit, which was supported largely by the international public policy-making community. The summit was instrumental in the creation of a UN commission on sustainable development to provide a new co-ordination mechanism for the implementation of Agenda 21. The commission was established in February 1993, having representatives from 53 countries.

Representatives from 183 nations attended the international conference on population and development, which was held in Cairo. It reached an agreement for an action plan to stabilize the human population by the year, 2020; and to provide greater equality for women along with improved reproductive health care. The world conference (4th) on women was held in Beijing in September 1995. This adopted a bill of Rights for women, and was ratified by about 160 countries by 1997. Same year, 1995 Berlin Climate Summit was held to strengthen the framework convention on climate change signed at the earth summit. It agreed that existing commitments to curb GHG emissions in developed countries were inadequate to meet the convention goals and wanted a protocol to strengthen the commitments. The member countries of the Berlin mandate sought to create the Global Environmental Facility (GEF), a body that would provide funds for global environmental projects.

In the same sequence of events the World Food Summit was held in Rome in November 1996. It committed to creating conditions for economic and social progress conducive to food security, poverty eradication and access to adequate food, sustainable increase in food production, human resource development, sustainable production and rural development, global cooperation in implementation and follow-up actions.

Effect of the Policies

It is a well-established fact that environmental efforts have tremendously increased at the global level by various institutions international, national, NGO's and other civic forums. After the Montreal Protocol the worldwide production of Chlorofluoro carbons (CFC's) has declined by 60 per cent in 1988, as observed by the World Watch Institute. The report ESPF of June 1997 found that the global environment has continued to deteriorate and that "significant environmental problems remain deeply embedded in the socio-economic fabric of countries in all regions."

The understanding of sustainable development as a concept and way of life may not necessarily emanate from global factors. There are various regional, local, sectored relationships between individual goals, institutional objectives that need to be taken into consideration. Sometimes it becomes difficult to draw a line between self-interest and common interest. In case the person involved is having limited assets in forms of material, land and money, he might not be able to preserve the principles of sustainable development.

Environmental Polices in India

Indian constitution is one of the very few of the countries of the world which refers clearly and specifically to the protection of environment. The chapter on directive principles of state policy and fundamental duties clearly speaks about the national commitment to protect and enhance the quality of the environment. Articles 48A and 51(g) to the 42nd Amendment laid the foundation for sustainable development. It says that, "State shall endeavour to protect and improve the environment and safeguard the forests and wildlife of the country (The Constitution of India, 1994). It is the duty of the citizens "to protect and improve the natural environment including forests, lakes, rivers and wildlife and to have compassion for the living creatures." The 42nd Amendment also expanded the list of concurrent subjects by incorporating "Population Control and Family Planning" and bringing "Forest" and "Protection of Wild Animals and Birds" from the state list to the concurrent list. India also has a clearly articulated National Conservation Strategy and Policy Statement on Environment and Development (1992), Policy Statement for a abatement of pollution (1992), National Forest Policy (1988), and National Water Policy (1987) that are blue prints for state action.

Apart from constitutional provisions, there are more than 200 Central and State laws, which have been enacted from time-to-time that are for environment protection and its management. In the ensuing paragraph there is an over view of environmental regulation in India which enumerates only the main statutes on the national environment.

1. Water (Prevention and Control of Pollution), Act (1974) Art. 252(1).
2. The Air Prevention and Control of Pollution (1981) (Art. 253).
3. Water (Prevention and Control of Pollution less Act, 1977).
4. Environment (Protection) Act, (1986) (Art. 253).
5. The Public Liability Insurance Act (1991).
6. National Forest Policy (1988).
7. The Wild Life (Protection) Act (1972), Art. 252 (1).

There are various other major institutions, which have been established to deal with pollution control. There is a Department of Environment (1980), which was later integrated into the ministry of Environment and Forests (1985) to recognize explicitly the pivotal role that environmental conservation must play in sustainable development. The Union Ministry appoints expert committees to undertake environmental impact assessments of projects that require approval of agencies such as the Central Water Commission, Central Electricity Authority, Planning Commission and Public Investment Board. Laws are implemented through the ministries and agencies of the Central and State Governments. Apart from State Departments of environment and the Central and State pollution control boards, institutions such as the National Waste Lands Development Board (1985), National Afforestation and Eco-Development Board (1992), Central Ganga Authority (1985), Central Zoo Authority (1991) and Animal Welfare Board of India (1962), play an important role in implementing environmental policies and laws. In areas like solid wastes, water treatment, health, and sanitation, which pertain to common amenities the state governments, municipalities the state governments, municipalities, and panchayats (village/local governments) play a significant role in preserving the environment.

Women Empowerment as Logic

In this century, there has been incessant change, technological revolution and innovation, but the most unprecedented presence has been of women as contributor to all areas of economic and social life as farmers, entrepreneurs, traders, workers, home-makers and mothers. Women are continuously striving forward and taking positions of influence in increasing numbers in communities, schools, workplaces, government, media, and in virtually all those areas which were considered to be men's fields. Women share the labour, rather put in more hours of work along with their household duties and yet get an unequal share in the fruits of labour due to continuous discrimination. They are the major chunks in the worlds' poor and continue to get discriminated in basic amenities in education, health and employment. The following points, which gained consensus in the fourth world conference on women in Beijing 1995:

- Women will remain second class citizens in the absence of access to the economic, political and social resources and levels of decision-making enjoyed by men;
- Women are central to development, particularly in developing regions; the wider objectives of human developments and peace cannot be achieved without eliminating discrimination against women.

There has to be thinking on the past inequalities and recognition of the fact by the policy makers that their decisions affect women and men differently. Women must be involved at all levels in efforts to eradicate poverty, promote peace and achieve sustainable development.

The Beijing Declaration reiterated in its platform for action that: "The continuing environmental degradation that effects all human lives often has a more direct impact on women. Women's health and their livelihood are threatened by pollution and toxic wastes, large-scale deforestation, desertification, drought and depletion of the soil, with a rising incidence of environmentally related health problems and even death reported among women and girls. Those most affected are rural and indigenous women, whose livelihood and daily subsistence depends directly on sustainable eco-systems."

Poverty and environmental degradation are closely interrelated. While poverty results in certain kinds of environmental stress, the major cause of the continued deterioration of the global environment is the unsustainable patterns of consumption and production, particularly in industrialized countries, which are a matter of grave concern and aggravate poverty and imbalances.

Sustainable development and economic growth that is both sustained and sustainable are possible only through improving the economic, social, political, legal and cultural status of women. Equitable social development that recognizes empowering the poor, particularly women, to utilize environmental resources sustainably is a necessary foundation for sustainable development.

The concept of sustainable development has been defined by various institutions and academicians in various ways but the meaning of sustainable development by World Bank has been quoted as "to a large degree, environmental management should be seen as a means of attaining the wider objectives of sustained economic growth and poverty alleviation, concern about environmental matters and developing the capacity to implement the sound practices for environmental management are needed to reconcile and, where appropriate, make tradeoffs among the objectives of growth, poverty alleviation and sound environmental management."[16]

> "Poverty of people and of countries is thus a major cause of environmental degradation. That makes it essential if environment degradation is not to become completely unmanageable, to devise policies oriented toward economic growth, with special emphasis on improving the incomes of the poor. Nevertheless economic growth may also destroy the environment and further jeopardize the already tenuous lives of the poor. Thus growth is imperative for alleviating poverty; it may also adversely affect the poor and the environment if inadequate attention is paid to the poor and their needs."[17]

> "So the idea behind the conservation of natural resources is the preservation of the limited stock of

> natures goods in such a way that the access of the coming generation to these resources is not in any way diminished than what we enjoy today. The use of present natural resources should be such that the access and right of future generations is secured. The Brundtland Report defined Sustainable Development as "Development that meets the needs of the present generation without compromising the ability of the future generations to meet their own needs."[18]

There are definitely limits to growth of material consumption if the human welfare has to be sustained in the long run and the only way it can be done is to see that there is no depletion of natural resources base. If the objective of development has to be met it is important to maintain the balance.

Between the natural resources as well as the man-made resources, if man uses natural resource he can substitute it or replace it to a very minimum degree. Once forests are cut, they can be planted again but the flora and fauna, which is lost with the forest cover, is lost forever. The resources, which can be renewed, are also exhaustible in the sense that the rate of exploitation may exceed much more than their replenishment. There may occur continuous irreversibility that may lead to a great loss of total human welfare. For example, green house effects, oxygen layer depletion, extinction of species at an alarming rate, impact on climate etc. These are some of the size able impacts, which may totally herald the bio-diversity and crop patterns of the world over.

It is evident, so far that role of women in agriculture activity is much larger than it seems. They are in a constant interaction with environment and have a holistic ecological understanding of forests, land etc., which in term leads to their naturally inherited knowledge of regenerating the eco-system as a whole. It is the interrelatedness and interdependence between various material features of nature, and between nature and human existence and sustenance, that marks the women perspective in ecology as very significant. This in term makes our micro study of this region not only important but also indispensable for the understanding of this Himalayan region.

The issue of empowerment of woman or equal opportunities for men and women is fast gaining centre stage in order for social advancement to take place. It has hitherto been observed in the past that the rights of woman especially in rural areas to manage local environment have been undermined or ignored while simultaneously it has also been seen that whenever the efforts have taken place to promote women in environment and development, the movements have succeeded tremendously despite initial marginalizing attitude of the governmental agencies. The latest example of this can be the 'Green Belt Movement ' in Kenya by Wangari Maathai who was the Noble Prize winner for the year, 2004.

The extent of women's right to local environment is roughly associated with two pre-conditions, one the citizenship rights of the women and second, their right to contribute to the sustainability of the local environment to which they have contributed for years and on which they are dependent for their livelihoods. Finally, towards the end of this study the extent of the role of women in deciding the sustainability of local environment regarding the future of local social, environmental, political and economic rights of women in the state of Himachal Pradesh especially in Shimla will be evaluated.

Presently, Himachal Pradesh is comprised of 12 districts having an area of 55,673 sq. kms with a population of 60.8 lakhs according to the census report of 2001.

The decennial population growth rate during 1991-2001 is 17.5 per cent; sex ratio is at 970 per thousand, density

109 persons per sq. km and literacy rate stands at 77.1 per cent. The rural population of Himachal Pradesh is 54.8 lakhs where as urban is 6 lakhs. In the total population female population is 29.9 lakhs. The contribution of women in agriculture sector is about 67 per cent of the total labour force. Since the economy of Himachal is agricultural based, this is a contribution bigger than it seems because, generally the agricultural activity, which women folk are performing on a household land, does not automatically ensure their share in the income from the agricultural produce. Consequently leading to minimal or no say in the decision-making whether at the household level or at the level of institutions at the local rural level i.e. Gramsabha, Panchayats etc. So, their problems generally remain unaddressed. When it comes to the level of social investment in the form of various poverty alleviation programmes which invariably remain gender blind leaving a poor, women poorer when she suffers from the lack of access to infrastructure, productive inputs, education, training and nurturing of children further constraints her mobility.

The Beijing, Declaration in 1995,[19] "ensures women's equal access to economic resources, including land, credit, science and technology, vocational training, information, communication and markets, as a means to further the advancement and empowerment of women through the enhancement of their capacities to enjoy the benefits of equal access to these resources, inter alia, by means of international cooperation."

It further reiterates that it requires a strong commitment on the part of Governments, international organization and institutions at all level.

It seems obvious that economic development, social development and environmental protection are inter-dependent and mutually reinforcing components of sustainable developments, which is the framework of its efforts to achieve a higher quality of life for all people. It further emphasizes that empowering the poor, particularly women living in poverty, to utilize environmental resources sustainable to be a necessary foundation for sustainable development. Above mentioned perspective is reflected to a very minimum extent in the government policies and programmes. An effort will also be made by this study to see how much gender perspective is reflected in the system by work done through government and non-government agencies in the areas of women empowerment.

It is a ground reality that there are many priorities for women and environment emerges as just one of the many processes that is needed to bring about empowerment in rural women. The strategy of women coming together for environmental concerns can resolve many priorities and issues. Generally, economic development is considered equivalent to empowerment and in the process all other issues get pushed aside. Women mostly believe in progressing step by step, since such a method also provides enough opportunities for bearing and reflection. Therefore, it is important that a women's empowerment process is created where there is judicious distribution of their work and responsibilities at both levels; the family and society.

The different aspects (women earning power, economic role, outside the family, literacy and education, property rights and so on) may at first sight appear to be rather diverse and disparate. But what they all have in common is their positive contribution in adding force to women's voice and agency—through independence and empowerment.[20] The diverse variables identified in the literature thus have a unified empowering role. This role has to be related to the acknowledgement that women's power-economic independence as well as social emancipation can have far reaching impacts on the forces and organizing principles that govern divisions within the family and in society as a whole, and can, in particular, influence what are implicitly accepted as women's entitlements."[21]

So, the question is of women empowerment gaining popularity for its pluralism, diversity and for its potential to involve within diverse contexts. The struggle on the growth of women empowerment is rooted in the struggle for basic human rights. The transition from feudalism to capitalism ushered in notions of freedom free competition and free labour when this transition was taking place in the various parts of the world it gave the peasant and the labouring class the vision of the right to liberty and equality. However, this process has completely by passed women. It is through these processes that multiple vision of women liberation started getting articulated from liberal feminism to socialist marxist feminism to ecological, Gandhian, Christian, Islamic, Buddhists feminism as well as radical and anarchists feminism. There have been very different perspectives and various views and philosophies about women's struggle. These different shades of women's movements world over are based on and originate from the theory and practice of patriarchy. These all movements have stood against each other and at another level complemented each other, giving a new lease of life to the women's movement all over the world.

Women empowerment as concept is a continuously evolving doctrine, a belief system, a body of knowledge and practice, thoughts and action. It is a process of producing meaning and creating new representation of women hood—the individual and the collective identity of women. It is also recognition of discrimination and unequal treatment in social, cultural, religious, political and economic institutions. The struggle of women today is to achieve equality, equity, dignity and freedom of choice, to be able to control their bodies and lives.

Objectives of the Study

1. To examine the socio-economic profile of the rural women.

2. To examine the extent of social empowerment of rural women.
3. To examine the extent of political empowerment of rural women.
4. To examine the role of NGOs and GOs to bring about women empowerment.
5. To examine the relation between environment and women in rural areas.

To elaborate the objectives further more apart from the organizations active in Shimla and surrounding areas, it is the women in question of Shimla Rural who will be the focus of the study. The gender related differences, distribution of responsibilities and resources for survival within the households their access to administrative machinery, their understanding of political system, environment as an integral part of their life, role of Panchayati Raj Institutions in understanding issues related to women and environment will be dealt with.

It will also try to highlight the women's unequal and declining access to land and the barriers they face in poverty, property rights, control of resources etc. In the ensuing research the focus will also be on escalating ecological degradation and the burden borne by the rural women. These are some of the issues to be taken up in the data collection with the help of a separate questionnaire.

Hypotheses

The extent of women empowerment will determine the sustainability of development in rural areas.

This study attempts to levelly provide an overview of women in rural Shimla, to address the issues of women empowerment, sustainable development vis-à-vis poverty, and marginalisation and government efforts. It also attempts a preliminary assessment of the new issues and to strengthen the efforts at voluntary level and state level and to draw up an action plan.

Methodology

The respondents are drawn from women at large in the rural area of Shimla. To facilitate the collection of data from various organizations, face to face interviews were conducted and also information provided by them in their records and annual reports etc., was utilized.

The questionnaire was pre-tested in Shimla before being finalized. Data was collected from primary sources as well as secondary sources i.e. Annual Reports and other documents. Field visits to the offices of various organizations were conducted and discussions were held for the final report. The questionnaires meant for the rural women respondent are mainly from Shimla (Rural). The respondents were from 10 villages of Shimla (rural). After adopting the technique of random sampling about 200 women were short-listed from the rural households in these panchayats. Earlier we thought the criteria of choosing women respondent should be from rural poor households. But when the questionnaires were being pre-tested, it was revealed that the state of women was more or less the same whether they were from poor or not so poor backgrounds. Their access to resources was more or less the same irrespective of level of the family income. Hence, the criteria was fixed that the women should be from those households whose major share of income came from agriculture, or activities related to it. With a view to judge the level of empowerment viz., a viz. development, selection of backward pockets was made. Thus, the variegated performance of development especially the impact on women was determined.

The result was calculated with the help of averages and percentages in order to assess the women empowerment in this particular area.

In the end, a point is being emphasized that this study will be first of its kind especially in this region regarding issues of women empowerment and sustainable development. The data collected will lead us to new areas and hone our understanding of the prevalent, social, cultural, economic and political issues. The data collected may be of great use to many other agencies that are working on the similar lines-women, women education, women employment, social status of women, role of women in environment etc. The researcher with her team also observed and documented the various programmes at the village level where women gathered at a prearranged time to participate in variety of programmes (e.g. meeting of self-help groups or listen to consciousness raising speeches, plays and songs etc.)

Review of Literature

Berry's (2005)[22] work is on gender and social equity in community water management programmes. He approaches the problem by drawing upon his research on women's collective action in Himachal Pradesh and involvement with issues of gender and social equity in joint forest programmes. He calls attention to a number of issues, definition of a farmer i.e. landless men and women, although performing the vast majority of labour involved in the practices of farming are called labourers and housewives, whereas, landed men, named farmers, are then deemed the appropriate targets of agricultural programmes.

A case study by Tandon (2002)[23] proposes to reduce poverty through organizing poor, rural woman for sustaining and diversifying their livelihood options in the Eco-development zone of the Great Himalayan National Park, in Kullu district of Himachal Pradesh in India. He finds some noticeable change in women articulate and represents their interests, politically, even when they are by and large poor. He also reports that in one Panchayat (Graparle) out of 175 women not even one was literate, thus, making dependence on daily-wage labour to make ends meet really high.

A paper by Handy and Kassam (2004) [24] explored how a relatively small and isolated rural NGO, Chinmaya Rural Training Centre in the foot hills of Himalayas has been successful in the empowerment of rural women living in highly patriarchal and traditional societies. The qualitative findings from their interventions, gave credence to the fact that these women were indeed marginalised before coming into contact with this NGO.

Scheyvens[25] (2000) writes in her paper that, since in Himachal socially proscribed roles for women mean that women and girls have greater interaction with the natural environment than men, women's cooperation is needed if that natural resource base the resource upon which eco-tourism trade in dependent, is to be sustained.

Jose and Shanmugaratnam[26] contend that rural women constitute the invisible workplace, which keep the family and rural economy alive. But they and their labour often go unrewarded or under rewarded. Women represent half of the world's population and one-third of the official labour force, but they receive only 1 per cent of the world income and own less than 1 per cent of words property (UN conference, Copenhagen, 1980). He also finds that as men are drawn more and more into the folds of the market mechanism, women are increasingly left behind to tend to subsistence activities. A similar trend he reports from Himachal Pradesh when there is an increase in the proportion of women cultivation while the proportion of women agricultural labourers declined.

Maneja, 2002[27] in her thesis on women in Cameroon, the Kyrgyz Republic and Himachal Pradesh, India finds that there is certain complexity of women's agency because women's capacity to exercise choice, as well as to act, is determined by their particular social and cultural systems. Women's mobilization for economic empowerment can benefit from its engagement with technologies, but a minimum framework for capacity building needs to be set in place. She adds further that development interventions must work with women stakeholders to ensure that women's opportunities to utilize technologies are not inhibited by cultural dictates on seclusion, restriction on mobility or the unequal division of labour within the household.

Sen (2001)[28] in his essay on gender inequality, discovers that in the data thrown up by the Census of 2001 an interesting phenomena of a split India, "something of a social and cultural divide across India, splitting the country into two nearly contiguous halves, in the extent of anti-female bias in natality and post-natality mortality. He emphasizes the need to "take a plural view of gender inequality", and calling for a new agenda of action to combat and put on end to gender inequality.

Sen (2000)[29] in another essay on women's agency focuses on the fact that now the approach of the women movements has shifted from the "Welfarist"—to incorporate—the active role of women's to incorporate—the active role of women's agency. He observes that "men as well as women increasingly see both women, as active agents of change: the dynamic promoters of social transformations that can alter the lives of both women and men". He goes on to illustrates the reach and power of women's agency, particularly in two specific fields: (1) In promoting child survival and (2) in helping to reprieve fertility rates. Both these matters he finds have general developmental interest, that goes well beyond the pursuit specifically of female well being.

Aderinto (2001) [30] in his paper examines the constraints women face in rural Yoruba Community of Nigeria. In spite of the fact that women face similar kind of discrimination in terms of employment opportunities, access to social and productive resources, education, health status and family decisions, among others, there is one striking similarity between the Indian culture and Nigeria that is tacit preference for the education of the male- child. The paper concludes by suggesting some intervention programmes including the mobilization of resources to prepare women for leadership roles, and awareness creation about the problem facing women and indeed rural women in South-Western Nigeria.

Dereze and Sen (1998), on missing women find a link between literacy and gender relations, leading to relations being less patriarchal. Kerala is sighted as most obvious example along with Manipur, Meghalaya and Himachal Pradesh. It is further insisted that educational achievement, in the younger age groups has to become a more compelling political issue.

Richmond (2000)[31], discusses Meyers for his observation on excess female mortality not only in India but rest of the world. He offers to give useful example of Himachal Pradesh where female to male ratio has risen from 884 per 1000 males in 1991 to 912 in 1951 to 976 (second only to Kerala) in 1991. But the prediction of Meyers seems to have come true that sex ratio will dramatically fall. In spite of progressive social development indicators in the census of 2001, Himachal Pradesh, the sex ratio of female to male between the age group of 0-6 years has sharply declined i.e., 951 in 1991 census to 897 in 2001. So, the problem of excess mortality is not disappearing in Himachal Pradesh as suggested by Richmond but has come back with a vengeance.

Pandey (2005)[32], studies the state of present property rights of women and also the flames within 2004 Bill. She feels that inequalities will remain unless the entire coparcenary system is abolished totally since it has folds within folds of inequalities which cannot be death with in a piecemeal manner. She feels that gender equality in agriculture land can reduce not just a women's but her whole families risk of poverty, increase her livelihood options, enhance prospects of child survival, education and health, reduce domestic violence and empower women.

Sachs (2005)[33], discusses extreme cultural discrimination which women face, whether or not those biases are embedded in the legal and political system. He reports that in South Asia, young women facing extreme under nutrition with in the household even when there is enough household even when there is enough to go around. The women, often illiterate are poorly treated by in-laws and lack the social standing and perhaps legal protections to ensure their own basic health and well-being.

Devidson-Hunt (1998)[34] in this research study carried out in the Indian Himalayas in the State of Himachal Pradesh suggests that a household ownership of land and cattle resources generally corresponds to a household's increased use of village forests, but that the control and management of village commons is influenced strongly by socio-political village dynamics. He mentions that despite the predominate role of women in the utilization of village commons, not all women participate in the women's organization, the mahila mandal, that has gained substantial control of village resources i.e. common property resources, forests etc.

Jose and Sharmygaratnam (1990)[35] conducted this particular study on women's invisible work, in Trinandrum district, Kerala. The conclusions were much the same as they are even relevant today. According to them, women play a significant role in reproducing the rural household economy by their involvement in household production system. Their role seems to be under played. Their role seems to be under played by the conservational statistics and the ambiguity in classifying women's work. I support their one of the conclusion that declassing the society is not a sufficient condition, though necessary, in obtaining a balanced gender equation.

Strulik (2004)[36] in his paper looks into changes brought upon the local bodies by the political participation of women after 73rd and 74th Amendment. It was argued that by women's political participation i.e. women's prioritization and agenda sitting, women's working style or 'doing politics' gendered knowledge systems and gendered support systems, as well as gendered modes of interaction—the political space gets transformed. This paper gives special emphases to the role State officials support or non-cooperation, governmental guidelines. He adds that the meaning of "politics" and "the state" eventually is reshaped. He argues that the state intervention "women quota" can indeed become a weapon in the hands of women in struggle over the meaning of politics—a process which in turn reflexively influences the broader context of the social construction of gender.

Sainath (2004)[37] in his series on "How the Better Half Dies", he discusses about the stress on wives of rural areas of Andhra Pradesh as more and more men seek work as auto drivers on daily wage labourers, often without successes. He reports that for decades women keep farm and family going due to non-payments of debt, when they finally commit suicide, it goes unreported as farmers suicide as they are not even accepted as "farmers" they were just farmers' wives. Though on record there is about 1/5th of households which are women headed.

Duflo, and Jopalone (2004), also study the impact of reservation for women on the performance of policy-makers and on voter's perceptions of this performance. He finds women leaders at the rural local level to be less likely to be corrupt. The women's performance is much worse than established leaders. He thinks that it could be due to less experience, less education, and less likely to be literate. Voters may use these characteristics to form their opinion on women leaders.

Scope of the Study

The books, articles, papers, and various studies reviewed on different aspects of women empowerment provide us with a perspective on empowering women for the sustainable development and well-being. Various authors have highlighted in their writings on women empowerment through various related issues. This study will be a link in a series of these studies and women empowerment as a process to inter link women, their life and development in rural areas. This work will explicitly intend to contribute to identification of areas, which need attention by the policy making as well as governance and NGOs working in these areas.

REFERENCES

1. *The Millennium Development Goals*, Report 2005, UN, New York, 2005.
2. Sen, Gita, UNACC, Inter Agency Committee on Women and Gender Equality, 1999.
3. Batliwala Srilatha, *What is Female Empowerment*, Paper Presented in Seminar on Female Empowerment and Demographic Process, Moving Beyond Cairo, International Vision, for the Scientific Study of ....
4. *Idem.*
5. Batliwala Srilatha, *ASPBAE Defining Women Empowerment – A Conceptual Framework*, Fourth World Conference on Women. Beijing, Sept. 1995.
6. Sabine de Rooij, Institutional Capacity for Rural Women's Empowerment, Electronic Journal of Polish Agriculture Universities, 2005, Vol. 8, Issue-3.
7. Page and Czuba, *Journal of Extension*, Oct, 199, Vol. 37, No. 5.
8. *National Policy for the Empowerment of Women* – 2001 – 'India-Source' Department of Women and Child Welfare.
9. Towards Equality, 1974 and Highlighted in the National Perspective Plan for Women, 1988-2000, Platform for Action, Five Years After – An Assessment.
10. Bannerjee, N.K., *Challenging the Patriarchal Ethos of Society had never been the Agenda of the Indian State*, 1998.
11. Krishanmurthy Rajan, *Gender Issues in Agriculture and Rural Development Policy in Asia*, TAO, RAP Publication, 1995.
12. Gupta Kasturi Menon (W & E) *Attaining the MDG in India*, The Role of Publication and Service Delivery, 2004.

13. *India:* Report by Government of India to United Nations Questionnaire on Implementation of the Beijing Platform for Action, Jan, 2005.

14. *Idem.*

15. Women's Human Rights net Association for Women's Rights in Development (AWID).

16. World Bank (1987), "Environment, Growth and Development", *Development Committee*, World Bank, Washington DC.

17. World Bank (1988), "Environment and Development", *Development Committee*, World Bank, Washington, DC.

18. World Commission on Environment and Development, 1987, p. 8.

19. Rao, Lakshmi and Krishna, (2000), *loc.cit.*

20. Sen Amartya, *Development as Freedom*, Oxford University Press, New Delhi, 1990, 2000, p. 191.

21. *Ibid.*, p. 192.

22. Berry, Kim, *Gender and Social Equity in Community Water Management*, University of North Carolina at Ashenvile, 2005, not yet a fully developed paper.

23. Tandon, Vinay, 2002, *Getting Women to Choose-case Study on* "Sustainable Livelihoods and Poverty Alleviation, " Mountain Forum E. Consultation for the UNEP/Bishek Global Mountain Summit.

24. Handy and Kassam, *Femida and Jennary Kassam*, A Paper Presented at ISTR Conference, Toronto, Canada, July, 2004.

25. Scheyvens Regina, "Promoting Women's Empowerment through Involvement in Ecotourism." *Experiences from the Third World, Journal of Sustainable Tourism*, Vol. 8. No. 3, 2000.

26. Jose Darley and N. Shanmugaratnam, *The Invisible Work Force; Women in the Traditional Farming Systems of Kerala*, Southern India, 1999.

27. Aster Claire Maneja, *A Thesis, Women, Weaving and the Web: An Analysis of Rural Indian Women's Agency in Attaining Economic Empowerment*, George Town University, Washington D.C. 2002.

28. Sen Amartya, *Many Faces of Gender Inequality: An Essay, Frontline*, India's National Magazine from the Publication of the Hindu, Vol.18, Issue–22, Oct. 27- Nov. 09, 2001.

29. Sen Amartya, *Development as Freedom*, Oxford University Press, pp. 189-203, 2000.

30. Adeinto, Abideen Aderinto, *Subordinated by Culture: Constraints of Women in Rural Yoruba Community*, Nigeria, Nardic Journal of African Studies 10 (2) 176-187, 2001.

31. Richmond, Julius, *Excess Female Mortality in India: The Case of Himachal Pradesh,* Paper in American Journal of Public Health, September, Vol. 90, No. 9, 2000.

32. Pandey Shruti, 2005, *Property Rights of Indian Women*, www. co.za/ Conference, Downloded from internet.

33. Sachs Jeffrey, (2005). *The End of Poverty*, Penguin Books.

34. Hunt Kerril - Davidson, (1998), *Class, Gender and the Commons in the Indian Himalayas*, in the Sustainability in Fountain Environments John Sinclair, Fibret Berkes and James Gardner, Downloaded from Internet.

35. Jose Darleys, and N. Sharmgaratnam, 1990. *The Invisible Work Force: Women in the Traditional Farming System of Kerala*, Southern India, Downloaded from Internet.

36. Strulik Stefanie, (2004). Women—Panchayat—Electives at the *Interface of State and Village Politics*, Paper on the 18th European Conference on Modern South Asia Studies at Land University, Sweden.

2

Socio-Economic Profile of Rural Women

The notion of sustainable development has been defined, as the process of development, which would satisfy the needs of the present without compromising the ability of future generations to meet their own needs.[1] The significance of women perspective in policy-making for the effective natural resource management has hold of its own especially in rural areas. The need for pro-active participation by women is increasingly felt to fully realize the concept of sustainable development. It's highly importunate to take into consideration the women constituent in the articulation of local natural resource management plans so their successful implementation is ensured. It is noted in many studies[2] that any imbalance in the surrounding environment tends to influence men and women differently because of the gender division of work, roles and responsibilities in our patriarchal societies. Since women in an agricultural economy like India have a closer relationship with environment, indicators like literacy of women, access to information and knowledge, patriarchal system of the society, property rights, her invisibility in work done within and outside home, extent of participation in decision-making at all levels beginning from personal, family and community have an important bearing on sustainable development.

The socio-economic conditions play a pivotal role in constructing the physical environment and behaviour of an individual. The socio-economic status defines the levels of interaction with the rest of the environment in the society. Women in rural areas have specific assigned socio-economic duties, which keep them closer to the environment and hence make them ambassadors designate to preserve environment. Their everyday chores include i.e., collection of water, fuel, fodder; maintenance of kitchen garden, maintenance and protection of farmland, care of dairy animals and their products; household based work, to name a few, makes their relationship very special and close to the nature. In this part of the questionnaire many questions were asked, for example, age, caste, education, occupation, property, livestock details and family related information.

Age

The women in this study range between the age groups of 18 to 65 years; most women were married and lived with their husbands. The following table will be able to give us a clear picture.

Table-2.1
Age of Respondents

Age 18 to 35 years	105	52.5%
36 to 45 years	59	29.5%
46 to 65 years	36	18%
Total	200	100%

The age structure of the population on the one-hand expresses demographic dimensions of development, and on the other delineates the challenges for development. The growth of female population in the reproductive age group (15-44 years) in both absolute and relative senses reinforces the need for levels of investment in health, nutrition and related areas. In 2000,[3] estimated 47.4 per cent of the total female population was in the category of reproductive age women. This is also the age group, which raises questions on provisions for productive employment and opportunities for gainful participation in economic activity.

All women who were taken as respondents did household work as well as agriculture and related activities.

Table-2.2

Whether Below Poverty Line (BPL) or not

Category	*No.*	*Percentage*
From BPL list	51	25.5%
Non-BPL listed	149	74.5%

In Table 2.2 it is seen that 25.5 per cent of the women were from BPL household which were identified to be included in the Below Poverty Line list which is popularly known as IRDP list, some of the women reported that not all of the deserving were included in the list. In some cases the poorest never made it to the list hence, could never avail of the rural development programmes i.e. Swarnjayanti Yojana and earlier Integrated Rural Development Programme (IRDP). In a study[4] done earlier 90 per cent of the people believed that there were massive irregularities in the identification of IRDP list, which sets the tone for implementation of development programmes.

Table-2.3

Caste of Respondents

Category	*No.*	*Percentage*
From BPL list	51	25.5%
Rajputs	107	53.5%
SCs	87	43.5%
STs	3	1.5%
OBCs	3	1.5%
Total	200	100%

Caste

The findings in the Table 2.3 show that 53.5 per cent of the respondents were Rajputs and 43.5 per cent were Scheduled Castes. About 13.1 per cent of the total population of HP comprises of Schedule Caste. There are only 1.5 per cent of Schedule Tribes, whereas the female population is 29.9 lakhs according to the latest census report of the total 60.8 lakhs. It will also be pertinent to mention that of total population of HP 91.1 per cent lives in rural areas. The distribution of caste here is used as demographic indicators.

Education

Literacy and education are important tools for economic development, effective participation in decision-making and women empowerment. It is seen in those countries that have invested heavily in education that the quality of life and human development indicators have shown steady improvement and sustainable growth in all sectors. Sweden[5] has the highest proportion of women in decision-making positions both at the national and local levels. This is not surprising, perhaps, since in Swedish political parties there is a 50 per cent quota system for women. Swedish women tend to be more educated than Swedish men, and therefore, more likely to become public sector decision makers. Jamaica too is similar to Sweden where majority of women are well-educated and enter public sector. So it appears from the-above diverse examples that better educated women move into the roles of decision makers with ease.

The literacy rate of a community indicates the level of education facility available to the population. (See Table 2.4)

According to 2001 figures, the male literacy rate increased to 85.3 per cent and that of female to 67.4 per cent while the overall rate increased from 63.86 to 75.91 per cent. The growth rate in literacy[6] (NCW, 2004) from

Table–2.4
Level of Education

Category	*Below V*		*VIII and below*		*X and below*		*XII and below*		*Graduate*		*Illiterate*	
Below V and below	*No.*	*%*	*No.*	*%*	*No.*	*%*	*No.*	*%*	*No*	*%*	*No.*	*%*
	33	16.5	21	105	64	32	28	14	1	0.5	53	26.5

1981 to 2001 witnessed the growth rate of 34.65 per cent, however, the growth in the nineties slowed down than the previous decade, because of wider base after impressive growth results accumulated. The growth rates for female have shown better attainment than their male counterparts, yet in absolute terms, females are less literate than males. The gender gap in literacy stands at 17.9 per cent in H.P. and 17.1 in Shimla district. The literacy growth rate for the state in 1991-2001 period has been 13.27 per cent, while for female this growth rate has been 15.95 per cent. The achievements at the primary education level are almost diluted by the high rates of dropouts in the secondary and higher secondary level. H.P.[7] has one of the lowest dropout rates, 28 per cent though there is wide gap between girls dropouts in rural to urban areas. The gender gap in rural H.P. is 18.8 per cent whereas in urban H.P. is just 7 per cent.

Table–2.5
Level of Education of Respondents

Category	*Below V*		*VIII and below*		*X and below*		*XII and below*		*Graduates*		*Illiterate*	
Below V and below	*No.*	*%*	*No.*	*%*	*No.*	*%*	*No.*	*%*	*No*	*%*	*No.*	*%*
	33	16.5	21	10.5	64	32	28	14	1	0.5	53	26.5

Of the total of our respondents 26.5 per cent are illiterate. Here it may also be reported that illiterate came from the older age group of women, whereas younger women were almost all either middle, matric or had completed +2 level. The female literacy was 20.23 per cent in 1971, which has risen to 68.08 per cent in 2001 census showing more than three fold increase in the literacy of females. The dropout rates (I-VIII) for Himachal Pradesh stand at 28.1 per cent for girls against the all India figure of 60 per cent.[8]

Even a cursory examination of data from Rajasthan and Himachal Pradesh demonstrates that low rates of literacy in the former and relatively high rates of literacy in the later do not occur in isolation from other factors. A host of social indicators, including infant mortality, poverty, fertility, female participation in the labour force, and child vaccinations, show that women of H.P. enjoy higher level of well-being than those of Rajashtan.[9]

Occupation

The economic empowerment of women, their work participation is an important constituent towards measuring the gender equality or inequality. The per capita income continues to be the sole indicator of the economic well-being of the people, the gender deficient data makes it unable to estimate the per capita income of women in the state, a data gap if examined from a gender prism. In rural areas women generally have domestic chores and agriculture related activities as occupation. The economic set-up of a family in Himachal Pradesh is distinguished by land holdings that are directly inherited by sons or other male family members. Women are excluded from having any ownership rights over land or property. The rights are in place but rarely exercised. Himachal Pradesh being an agriculture based state the access to land certainly means control over material or economic resources, it being the single most mode of production. The women work on the land but rarely own it. However by doing so they add to the family income but remain dependent on their husbands or other male members of the family for looking after her needs i.e. especially those which have to be addressed economically.

Table–2.5
Choice of Occupation

Category	*No.*	*Percentage*
Agriculture	187	93.5%
Animal Husbandry	159	79.5%
Daily wages	13	6.5%
Shop (small)	3	1.5%
Anganwari	6	3%

From the Table 2.5, it is revealed that 93.5 per cent of the respondents belonged to a family whose main occupation was agriculture. Agriculture and animal husbandry were two occupations carried on simultaneously in most of the households though 6.5 per cent were also daily wagers. Agriculture accounts for 30 per cent of the state's net domestic product and provides employment to about 71 per cent of its residents. The annual growth rate of the State during 1999-2000 was 58 per cent against India 64 per cent.

In the agriculture sector women are engaged in low-skill activities, such as seed application, post-threshing, storing and, looking after crops in the slack season, and are engaged in livestock farming (Raj Kumari, 1989). The quality of women employment is poor in the State. This supports the finding that the effective per day wage rates for all wage-work (agriculture and non-agriculture work) for females is Rs. 18.6 at least 40 per cent lower than the male workers (Rs. 31.2).[10] It may also be added that female cultivators in Shimla district constitutes 83.9 per cent whereas male cultivators are only 50.5 per cent.

It is evident from the Table 2.6 that 46 per cent of our respondents owned land about 4 to 6 bighas only whereas there are 5.5 per cent of households who claimed to have no land, which is a matter of concern.

Table-2.6
Land Owned by the Family

Category	*1 to 3 bighas*		*4 to 6 bighas*		*6 bighas to more*		*Don't know*		*No Land*	
	No	*%*	*No*	*%*	*No*	*%*	*No*	*%*	*No*	*%*
	92	46	36	18	39	19.5	18	9	11	5.5

Himachal Pradesh has 16,997 inhabited villages and over 90 per cent of the population lives in rural areas. Population of Shimla district is 722,502 whereas rural population is 76.8 per cent of it.[11] According to the Annual Administrative Report[12] about 84 per cent of the farmers have less than two hectares of land, while 16 per cent have over between 2 to 10 hectares. In the case of Scheduled Castes, 93 per cent of the farmers own less than two hectares, and cultivate 70 per cent of total area sown. In Shimla district alone 83.9 per cent are women cultivators, agricultural women labourers are 2.6 per cent, in household industries their representation is 0.9 per cent, whereas the work participation rate (main + marginal) amongst rural women is 51.8 per cent. This shows that large numbers of women are marginal workers and no effort is being made to shift them to activities related to income generation. The overall quality of women employment is abysmally low.

Table-2.7
No. of Family Members

2 to 5 members		*6 to 9 members*		*9 and more*	
No	*%*	*No*	*%*	*No*	*%*
82	41%	77	38.5%	41	20.5%

Size of the Family

The respondents had comparatively medium families. 41 per cent of them were in the category of 2 to 5 family members. Average household size in Shimla district is 5.0, the findings reiterates this fact. According to the latest census of H.P.[13] 15 to 59 years fall in the category of working age population and are 57 per cent. Child population (0-6 years) is 16.2 per cent of the total population, whereas Shimla district individually has 953 sex ratio in rural areas. In urban areas in the same category it falls drastically to 832/1000 males. This calls for the debate and research in female foeticide in urban areas. The result of fertility decline is manifested in the shrinking child population in the age group 0-6 years. The drastic decline in the number of such young age groups by 8.5 per cent in the last decade is attributed to fall in fertility.[14] This will be elaborated more while discussing the next Table 2.8.

Table-2.8
Number of Children

No Children		*1 Child*		*2 Children*		*3 Children*	
No.	*%*	*No.*	*%*	*No.*	*%*	*No.*	*%*
8	4%	23	11.5%	75	39.5%	40	20%

4 Children		*5 Children*		*6 Children*	
No.	%	No.	%	No.	%
34	17%	9	4.5%	7	3.5%

39.5 per cent of our respondents had two children. There is also a category of 1 child and no child followed by 11.5 per cent and 4 per cent. The respondents who were in the category of no children were either not married or newly married, respondents in the second category were also in the age group that they could have a second child. It was also found that in rural areas two children was the norm especially amongst the new couples that had been married for 10 years or less. Consideration for a male child further increased the number of children. Woman who had 5 or 6 children were mostly in the older age group. They emphasized that about 20-25 years ago having 5 to 6 children was normal. And also that family planning was not so popular than in rural areas. This point will be elaborated further at a later stage. There has been a fall in fertility among women in all ages between 1981 and 1999 (SRS).[15] Even the NFHS (2002)[16] reports almost negligible women in the age group of 44-49 years. Child bearing coming immediately after marriage is mainly in the age group of females between 20-24 and 25-29. Which is about 47 and 30 per cent of the total births, in the whole reproductive span of women.

Table-2.9
Property Owned by the Respondent

Do you own any property	*Yes*		*No*	
	No	*%*	*No*	*%*
	26	13%	174	87%

The above question was purposely asked to the respondents to see whether women in rural areas actually owned any property or not. The women who owned some land or house were 13 per cent of the total respondents. As Sen[17] puts it that ownership of property can also be very unequal. Even basic assets such as homes and land may be very asymmetrically shared. The absence of gains to property cannot only reduce the voice of women, but also make it harder for women to enter and flourish in commercial, economic and even some social activities. Mukund[18] (1999) argues that women, rights to inherit, own and control property are determined primarily by the values and norms which are socially acceptable, as well as the mechanisms of intra-household decision-making and distribution. Bina Agarwal[19] (1994: 11) however cautions that, "in this emphasis on the ideological, the possible material basis of this subordination, or the dialectical link between the material context and gender ideology, is seldom recognized. And, culture is often characterized as 'given' rather than in the process of constant reformulation, or as an arena of contestation."

Though the researcher went with a mindset quite assured that no women would own any property, but was surprised at the revelations, so the connecting question followed.

Table-2.10

Who Gave you this Property?

Sr. No	*Question*	*No*	*%*
1.	Given to you by your parents	13	6.5%
2.	Given to you by your in laws or husband		
3.	Inherited after the death of husband	13	6.5%

In the Table 2.10, it is indicated that their parents either gave women who owned property i.e. 6.5 per cent or they inherited it after their husbands had expired i.e. 6.5 per cent. The research in this area of Himachal Pradesh has shown that the prevailing gender ideologies raise many obstacles for women to own property from their parental home. During the discussion it was also revealed that it was generally felt that a girl has to leave her parental home to another village or place after marriage it would not be possible for her to look after a piece of land in absence. Secondly, women also found the idea of owning property or land unthinkable if her husband was alive. Nobody could respond to a query satisfactorily that if it would not come handy in case of domestic discord or any untoward happening. It may further be added that 22 per cent of the households are women headed in HP.[20]

Dereze and Sen[21] add further that economic growth can positively influence the status of women through expanding opportunities for remunerative female employment, which often result in an improvement in the 'deal' that a woman receives within the family. But these influences, though fairly extensive in some cases, can be slow, and in great need of supplementation by more direct public action in pursuit of gender equity, focusing for instance on educational transformation women's ownership rights and political activism.

In the recent theories of gender in the third world have constantly debated that gender is not treated separately from other kind of difference but rather is constituted at the intersection of hierarchies such as caste and class.

Table–2.11

Whether a Woman's Prestige is Enhanced if she Brings Movable or Immovable Property from Parental Home

Do you think a women prestige is fairly enhanced in her in laws home if she brings some property with her?	*Yes*		*No*	
	No	*%*	*No*	*%*
	108	54%	92	46%

Improvement in Status of a Woman if Dowry is Brought

In response to the above question 54 per cent said yes reiterating the fact that material exchange during marriages is accepted and prevalent in the villages. Though it much depends on the economic status of the bride's family. The women also further added that since a girl does not get any share in the parental property, it was a good practice to give her something in cash and kind during her marriage. It is also a common practice that gifts are given to the girl and her family during the various festivals and when she bears children. Mukund[22] further argues that this has tremendous relevance even for contemporary society since this denies women access to the most important productive source in the Indian economy, viz, land.

Table–2.12

Whether had any Vocational Training

Have you taken any vocational training?	*Yes*		*No*	
	No	*%*	*No*	*%*
	42	21%	158	79%

From the Table 2.13 number of our respondent only 21 per cent seemed to have some kind of vocational training. It mostly constituted of either stitching clothes, two days workshops for growing vegetables, 5 days training of growing mushroom etc. There was only one women who had learned English Typing, that too she maintained was her own effort.

Consequent of the above question next question was asked related to whether they utilized this training to generate income.

Table–2.13
Earned Income as Consequence of Vocational Training

Have you been able to generate	*Yes*		*No*	
income as a result of this training?	*No*	%	*No*	%
	12	6%	27	13.5%
Stitching	3	1.5%		

The women who did stitching of clothes spent about 3 hours daily on this work in addition to their household and agriculture activities, which fetched them about Rs. 1,000 to Rs. 2,000 in a month. The women, who did knitting though a very small number, made about a pair of socks a day for about Rs. 30 to 40 per pair. They admitted that it was mostly a seasonal practice. Though many of them had received training to grow vegetables due to scarcity of water it was not pursued. There are various programmes run by the Government for rural development such as Indigination of Rural Education, Rural Indigination, Rural Poverty Alleviation Programmes, Swarnajayanti and Gram Swarojgar Yojna. Sampooran Grameen Rojgar Yojana (SGSY) and various other projects under its aegis have about 4,613 number of SHGs of which women's SHGs are only 390 out of which again only 158 SHGs have taken up economic activities. There is definitely need for improved coordination between Government departments, Non-government organizations, Panchayati Raj Institutions and private institutions to explore better opportunities for employment.

HP was a land of some rare handicrafts, and these goods were exported to overseas markets. In course of time, handicrafts such as pattus (sheep wool shawls) Thobis (goat hair items), Kasida (embroidery goods) and silver ornaments have almost vanished and the artisans have abandoned these skill-based vocations.[23]

The women respondents were further asked to elaborate on their daily routines. All of them reported that their day started with the break of the dawn. After cooking the daily meal, they often went to cowsheds to look after the cattle, after coming back at about lunch time they would again go to tend fields. Exchange of labour was common within household women and rare amongst the village as a community. Along with cooking, looking after the cattle, children rearing, tending the fields, they often had to go for fuel wood and fodder in nearby forests. When there was scarcity of water especially in summers they often had to go to a common natural source of fetching water for daily use. They have reported to be working round the clock except for an hour's rest after lunch. They mentioned that since young people especially boys do not want to work in fields and tend cattle, this has reduced the number of cattle people have and in turn reduced the quantity of manure. The exposure to the television had made young boys and girls unnecessarily over ambitious, which had little to do with the ground realities. They considered agriculture not lucrative enough to look after their inflated life requirements. This change had also seemed to have dwindled their relation and respect for environment which the earlier generation has.

With few exceptions almost all households had gas cylinder connection, but they used it scarcely, viz, for making tea for guests, boiling water in a small quantity, warming milk etc. Though fuel wood was reported to be used for making meals and warming water for baths etc. It is indisputable that it is women who go out in search of fuel and fodder. Although, there are various issues related to rural women and improvement in their status there is strong evidence of social cultural norms, which influence their position in the rural society. Due to patriarchal values women are considered workers of all household activities as well as other forms of work common to village life routine.

To end this part of the discussion a wrap up question was asked whether they ever evaluated their work in terms of money. Some of the respondents were almost wide-eyed at the change in perspective of looking at their work. Women who belonged to younger age groups were prompt to reply that if a labourer had to be hired to do the kind of work they did, he would have to be given at least Rs. 2000 per month with food. The researcher further probed whether they were actually given any sum of the money by selling of the produce or were they given anything in cash. The ready answer was that it was never expected and never given. Sometimes they sold fodder or fuelwood, which is the only earning they had. To conclude the discussion on the socio-economic profile, the picture that comes to mind of the women respondents is that most of them had no property; some of them know that they had property rights but never exercised for social reasons, most of them had 10th standard education especially of the younger age group, with almost no vocational training. They encouraged dowry in sub-dued tones for the reason that it was a kind of compensation to them for not getting anything from parental property. The younger age group women though seemed very enthusiastic to learn new skills but they invariably complained about the lack of information dissemination by the local institution and later in continuity of the programmes. Some of them said that they were very upbeat about growing vegetables but because of scarcity of water their plans could not really take off. A very encouraging picture that emerged was decline and control in fertility the reasons for which will be revealed more in ensuing chapters.

REFERENCES

1. 'Our Common Future (1987), the report of the World Commission on Environment and Development (WCED).
2. See Sachs, Carolyne E., (1996), *Gendered Fields, Rural Women, Agriculture, and Environment, Rural Studies Series,* Westview Press also Chakaravarti, Uma, (1993) Conceptualising Brahminical Patriarchy in Early India, EPW, April 3, p. 579.
3. Himachal Pradesh Development Report, 2005, *Planning Commission,* Government of India, Published by Academic Foundation, New Delhi.
4. Singh, Anupama (2006), *Bureaucracy at the Grassroots Level in India,* Kanishaka Publishers, p. 141.
5. *Women in Local Leadership,* Icweb2.loc.gove/annem/ ndfpedu/ features/women/equal.html. p. 103.
6. National Commission for Women (2004), *A Situational Analysis of Women and Girls in Himachal Pradesh.*
7. *Census of India* (2001).
8. Tenth Five-Year Plan (2002-07), *Planning Department,* Government of Himachal Pradesh.
9. Cohen, Alex, Arthur Kleinman, Bandetto Saraceno (2002), *World Mental Health Case Book,* Springer Publication, p. 183.
10. *Himachal Pradesh Development Report* (2005), pp. 194-95.
11. *Census of India,* 2001.
12. *Annual Administrative Report,* Department of Agriculture, HP 2001-02.
13. *Census of India,* 2001.
14. HPDR, *op.cit,* p. 86.
15. Statistical Reports (different volumes), *Sample Registration Systems* (SRS), Registrar General, India.
16. *National Family Health Survey* (2002).
17. Sen, Amartya (2001), Many Faces of Gender Inequality, Frontline, Volume 18-Issue 22, Oct. 27, Nov. 09, 2001.
18. Mukund, Kanakalatha(1999):'Women's Property Rights in South India', *EPW,* May 29, pp. 1352-58.
19. Agarwal, Bina in Mukund, *Idem.*
20. *Census of India,* 2001.

21. Dreze, Jean and Amartya Sen (1998), *India – Economic Development and Social Opportunity*, Oxford University Press, p. 194.
22. Mukund, *op.cit*, p. 1353.
23. HPDR, (2005), *op.cit*, p. 232.

3

Social Empowerment of Women

Women all over the world either independently or largely look after the families. Women are the provider for the family though their labour and effort may go unrecognized. It is important first to see the extent of their participation in decision-making at the household level to determine her control over the factors, which greatly influence her life within and outside the household. It is a well-accepted fact by theorists that increased participation in decision-making at the household level will lead to increase in participation at all other levels outside. In traditional societies like India where patriarchy rules the roost social equality will certainly lead to economic opportunity and personal rights. Most often women are deprived of human rights as a matter of tradition. In rural areas women generally do not have any role in income generation activities. Their contribution is mainly considered only in areas of household activities. Ramanathan (2004)[1] emphasises that women have multiple identities based on gender, caste, class, ethnicity and age; at any given point of time any one or combination of factors could oppress them. Family structures in developing countries like India manifest and perpetuate the subordinate status of women. There are several hidden social constraints that inhibit women's free choice of what they want to do. Women often internalize the traditional conception of their role as natural, thus inflicting an injustice upon themselves.

The most elementary form of division of labour is found on the basis of gender. In pre-historic times it seemed to have started from hunting and gathering bands to the most developed industrial societies having a definite criteria for men's work and women's work. With increase in the level of education and awareness in urban areas this marked line is challenged in households and workplaces but situation doesn't seem to mitigate in rural areas. Chatterjee (1985)[2] examines some of the factors, which are responsible for the inequality. Firstly, the division of labour between men and women, justified on the basis of women's child bearing function, has tended to restrict women in the domestic sphere and has limited access to participation and decision-making in all spheres of life. Secondly, inequality stems from mass poverty and general backwardness of the majority of the world population, caused by under-development. The unfavourable status of women is aggravated in many countries, developed and under developed, by de facto on discrimination on the basis of sex. And thirdly, the predominant economic analyses of labour and capital insufficiently trace the linkages between the economic productions, of women's work; women are not discriminated against because of their reproductive power.

The researcher with her team had attended various meetings of Mahila Mandals and Self-Help Groups, in which women discussed about their limitation to come to the meetings. The main reason was that there was nobody to attend to cattle and young children. Some of them said that even when their husbands were at home, they would not substitute for them even for a day, thinking its not part of their job at all. Secondly, man folk did not also like the idea of women going out, getting together and attending some meeting and some even thought that their thinking was being polluted. So mostly women came to these meetings but to the researcher's understanding with a sense of guilt. It's only the resolve of womenfolk, which has made SHGs and Mahila Mandals a success. It is true that without the power to work and earn a good income, their voice would be silenced. The first step towards it would be through social empowerment. Probably a real holistic solution lies in a holistic approach that deals with all other major interrelated issues of economic welfare, social justice, education, health and tradition.

National Policy for the 'Empowerment of Women'[3] mentions that Women Empowerment has been recognized as the sole issue in determining the status of women. The 73rd and 74th Amendments (1993) to the constitution of India have provided for reservation of seats in the total bodies of Panchayats and Municipalities for women. Social Empowerment of Women is given a separate mention in clauses 6.1 to 6.12, which is a credible achievement for women movements in concrete forms. Issues like education, health, nutrition, housing and shelter, environment, science and technology and women in difficult circumstances are included in the policy progress towards gender equality though these kinds of interventions ultimately raise issues of the sustainability of gains. If we take women empowerment as goal, social empowerment certainly provides an atmosphere so that the ultimate objective of gender equality seems achievable. Despite lack of voice in social issues, women belong to a household, which gives her shelter and protection from the outside anti-social forces. There are conflicting issues between men and women but there are common meeting grounds of mutual well-being too. So the approach of women empowerment has to be gender focused, which will be elaborated in ensuing paragraphs.

Of all the decision enumerated above it was the issue related to children's education, the respondents found most important. Second best comes the decision regarding sharing of household work with the rest of the family members. The selling and buying of property comes last in the list of their important decision.

Table–3.1
Decisions About Important Household Chores

	From the following which household decision you think are important	*Response* *No*	*%*
1.	Selling and buying of land or other property	86	43%
2.	Purchasing utensil, clothes or any other thing for your household	112	56%
3.	Sharing of household and other work	120	60%
4.	Related to children's educations	132	66%
5.	Related to children's sickness or any other	112	56%

The obvious corollary of the above question was whether their opinion is taken while taking the above-mentioned decision. Women's experience as well as response regarding the particular issue was not only mixed but women seemed rather unaware of their being as for how far they could go to influence the decisions. Looking after the household and childcare responsibilities is so much ingrained in the women's conscious and prevailing power equations within the households that even the conflicts arising out of it are questioned for their validity.

This formulation of power is concerned with ideology, and with patterning of behaviour. It prevents conflicts between dominant and subordinate groups by shaping attitudes, wants, needs and preference in such a way that both accept the existing order either because they can imagine no alternative to it or because they value it as divinely ordained or beneficial. Feminist analysis has shown how social rules, norms, values and practices play a crucial role in concealing the reality and pervasiveness of gender inequality and in defusing gender conflict. For instance, the reverence of mothers and motherhood conceals, and also serves as re-buttal, of the evidence of the exploitation, devaluation and exploitation that women face, as reported by Sompar and Kapur (2000).[4] No doubt the issue of gender subordination is complex as well as has linkages to social cultural, religious norms in the society which are well accepted and practiced for centuries. As some respondents also reported that if the permission for going out was related to some religious function i.e. Kirtans or Jagratas etc., the proposal would be more readily accepted than otherwise.

Table–3.2
Whether Their Opinion Taken

Category	*Response*			
Is your opinion taken while taking	*Yes*		*No*	
any of the above mentioned decision?	140	70%	60	30%

The respondents were asked whether their opinion was taken while taking the above decision. About 70 per cent of them agreed that they are part of the discussion but ultimately it's the man of the house whose decision prevails. It was also mentioned that in case of absence of father-in-law, mother-in-law took a more dominating role. Women's autonomy about participation in household decision-making has a direct impact on various other demographic health related problems, purchasing household items etc. These are also indicators to the fact that since she has no direct access to material assets how much her opinion matters. National Family Health Survey-2[5] asked women to report who in their household makes decision about the following: what items to cook, obtaining health care for herself, purchasing jewellery or other major household items etc. As was expected, ever-married women in India are most likely to participate in decisions about cooking: 71 per cent make their own decisions, purchasing jewellery or other household items (47%). Only 28 per cent all over India took decision on their own regarding their health. NFHS also reported that women's participation in household decision-making, alone or jointly with others, increases with age, suggesting that autonomy also increases with age. This finding is also quite similar to our finding where mother-in-law has more say in household decision-making. However, irrespective of the fact whether women have an opinion or not regarding children's education, they seemed most concerned that they get good education whether the sibling was a girl or a boy. It was also reported that generally when an extra hand was required it was the girl whose school was sacrificed not the boy's. There was also an incident in a village where a girl was to be married after finishing tenth standard but the plans of her marriage were terminated only at her own insistence that she wanted to study further and go to a college etc.

Table–3.3
Whose Decision Matters?

Category	*Response*	
	No	*%*
Husbands or father-in-laws	104	52%
Your own or women's opinion	96	48%

The rural women respondents were further probed as whose opinion ultimately influenced the final decision. As is clear in the previous table that 70 per cent women agreed to their opinion being taken in matters of household enumerated above. The 52 per cent of respondents agreed to that it was their husband or generally elders in case alive whose opinions and decisions mattered most. It was further clarified that mutual consent mattered but to an extent. Some women also mentioned that sometimes the opinion of school going teenage son would matter more, as they thought they were exposed to new ideas and interacted with semi-urban environment in schools. The need to earn independent incomes and to be able to influence the decision-making regarding issues related to their lives is increasingly felt. The need to elaborate this issue that how rural women can earn some income is a matter which should seriously be a part of development policies and further research.

Economic empowerment constitutes one of the fundamental building blocks in efforts towards the overall empowerment of women. Participation in formal economic activities on terms and conditions, which reflect the productive capacity of women, and their control over their own incomes, are some of the important dimensions of economic empowerment.[6] The goal of achieving the economic and social empowerment of women is enshrined in the Nairobi Forward Looking Strategies for the Advancement of Women (1985), the Jakarta Declaration for the Advancement of Women in Asia and the Pacific (1994) and the Beijing Declaration and the Platform for Action (1995).[7] These landmark declarations have definitely brought new beginning with them but their objectives needs to be translated to the grassroots level by various governments. The household industry, which is defined as a person who is doing some economic activity at home or close by and earning some income, forms only 1.4 of the total female workers.[8] It cries for the need for strong governmental policy intervention. About 16, 84, 157 females in HP fall in the category of non-workers according to the census what is again a matter of great concern.

Next in the line of social indicators are some questions, which were asked on Dowry system as it prevailed in Shimla (Rural).

Table–3.4
Dowry System

Category	*Response*			
	Yes		*No*	
Did you bring dowry at the time of	*No*	*%*	*No*	*%*
marriage or later?	134	67%	66	33%

The respondents were quite equivocal on this issue, 67 per cent agreed to have brought dowry at the time of marriage. They also added that gifts were also given at the first-born or at other special occasions like festivals etc. As it is clear from the Table 3.5 majority of who get dowry are of the view that it was given to them by their parents out of their own will. It seems to be a very good indicator for rural society. The boom of sudden increase in the availability of material goods seems to have caught cities like an epidemic is far removed from villages. The rural women said that parents gave to their daughter whatever they could; depending on their economic condition. It was also revealed that sometimes there used to be some social pressures to give more to their daughters just to show off to their in-laws that she was from a materially good background, which was also a factor to gain respect at the in-laws house.

Table–3.5
Whether Dowry was Demanded

Category	*Response*	
	No	*%*
Any pressure on your parents to give the dowry?	24	12%
Or did they on their own will give it?	110	55%

In the annual reports of HP State Women Commission no mention is made of cases received under dowry harassment. There is not even a category mentioning the word "dowry". Under the category "atrocities" on women 51 cases were received in Shimla, 2004. The role of such commissions comes into being only when some atrocity has been committed but even after talking to high officials and other officials at the women commission it was found that issue of dowry is not so prevalent in rural areas, though, it is gaining grounds in urban areas. It is also an accepted fact that generally, the rural people rarely demand dowry.

The respondent were further asked whether they were in favour of dowry or not, only 24.5 per cent were in favour of the view, that too for the reason that they have some right on the parental property which could be exercised to an extent in this way. Though unequivocally majority were not in favour of situation where dowry was demanded as a matter of custom.

Next in the chain of social indicators comes the question of son preference in Shimla (Rural).

Table–3.6
Preference for Son

Category	*Response*			
	No	%	*No*	%
Forced to produce a son?	82	41%	118	59%
After evaluating your own life and societal attitudes is your preference for daughter?	138	69%	62	31%
Having a daughter means having more material and immaterial responsibilities?	36	18%	164	82%
If allowed to choose you would go for son only?	64	32%	97	39%
			Both	
			39	19.5%

A significant finding of this study is that 59 per cent of the rural women admitted to not being forced to have a son, 41 per cent believed that there was some pressure on them to have a son. It may also be mentioned that sex ratio of Shimla (Rural) is 946 per thousand in comparison to 748 in Shimla (Urban), that is a difference of 198 girls, where as all India figure is 933 for all ages.[9] The sex ratio of children (0-6 years) has declined from 951 in 1991 to 896 in 2001, which calls for rethink over various socio-cultural, economic and health related issues. Changes in juvenile sex ratio[10] can be linked to the overall preference for the male child in many areas of HP. Strong male dominance in property transfer, focus on male centric rituals and kinship system, inadequate appreciation of women's economic contribution, absence of strong social reform movements, etc., have contributed to higher value of the male child among many communities in Himachal society. Mutharayappa (1997)[11] and his team reports that main findings of these studies i.e. NFHS, that India's total fertility rate would fall by about 8 per cent if gender preference were eliminated (because some couples with gender preferences would stop having children). They mention particularly about HP where they find that influence of son preference on fertility is stronger among literate woman than among illiterate women. This may occur simply because literate women are more likely to use modern conception to control their fertility or later pointing for sex selective abortions. A policy implication is that the Government can speed up the process by promoting the value of gender equality and by enhancing the status of women by increasing educational levels, media exposure, and opportunities to work outside the home for women.

In HP, sex selected abortion are rampant, has more substance than being just a statement. Richmond (2000)[12] strongly puts his case that women will tend to have longer life expectancies and their proportion of the population will exceed that of men, when men out number women, as they do in India and China as well as in other countries in South Asia and sub-Saharan Africa, the most parsimonious explanations is that human behaviour, in the form of severe gender inequalities, is the fundamental cause of excess female mortality and of a significant imbalance in the populations female to male sex ratio.

It may also be pertinent to mention that sex ratio in Himachal Pradesh was 884 per 1000 males in 1901, which increased to 976 in 1991, which was only second to Kerala. The census of 2001 has brought grim realities of lower female rates to the force especially in 0-6 years age group, having dropped to 897.[13] Another point of concern is that female mortality under 5 years has dropped from 86.6 thousand in 1992-93 to 42.8 per cent thousand in 1998-99.[14] In spite of improvement in Health and education levels the gap between males and females continues to rise. The economy is growing at the rate of 6.7 almost at par with rational growth rate 6.8 in 1998-99.[15] In addition to that there has been dramatic improvements of social well-being, improvements of social well-being, female literacy has almost jumped from 7.7 per cent in 1901 lowest in India to 68 per cent in sharp contrast to 54.35 per cent at the National Level. Why has sex ratio declined so rapidly during past one decade, what are the reasons responsible for it is not only a matter of debate but requires serious research and policy measures?

The respondents in the study were well-aware of the prevailing bias against the girl child, which has also led to answers than otherwise preferences. The number of children one had 5.0 per household in Shimla (Rural). The reason for having a number of children is not just adding working hands to the family but also there were cases where there were 3-4 daughters and mother was again on the family way. It speaks of the reality that the family was waiting for the male heir to their aspirations. The absence of sex determination clinic in rural areas has led to increase in the number of children one had. There were however 19.5 per cent of the respondents who wanted both boys as well as girls to be their siblings. The discussion on preference for son in HP can be concluded by observation made by Malhi[16] and her team. In her outcomes the fertility behaviour appears to be influenced by a strong desire to acquire a minimum number of at least two surviving sons. In the light of her finding, it appears that despite the declining fertility level in HP, further reduction in fertility may increasingly be more difficult to achieve unless there is a concomitant decline in the preference for male children. Since son preference is linked to women's status in society, there is an urgent need to bring about widespread structural changes to enhance the status of women in the State.

Table 3.8 gives us the information on the age of the respondents, the time they were first married. Under the first category of less than 18 years, are mostly those rural women who fall in the older age group, hence a tabulation that age of married women is rising. There are 44.5 per cent of women who got married between 19-21 years of age. These age groups seemed to be the most favoured age in the rural areas of Shimla. There are about 22 per cent who got married when they were 22 or 23 years of age. However, 5.5 per cent of the respondents got married at the age 24-27 years, considered though late for marriage in villages. The NFHS[17] also corroborates our finding that 38.2 per cent were married in Himachal at the exact age of 18 years. 67 per cent got married at the age of 20 years.

Table–3.8
Age at the Time of Marriage

Under 18 years		*19-21 years*		*22-23 years*		*24-25 years*	
No	*%*	*No*	*%*	*No*	*%*	*No*	*%*
56	28%	89	44.5%	44	22%	11	5.5%

These findings can be correlated to the fact that incidence and interest in education of girls is increasing in the rural areas as well. The enrolment of girls in school 6 to 14 years of age is 80-52[18] and dropout rate is 6.2 per cent. The retention rate is nearly 99 per cent at[19] primary level, which is a major achievement for the Government but the dropout rates has increased for girls at X and XI-XII levels. It was also observed and understood after the discussions with the rural women that they considered education to be very important for girls at the very initial level but their interests flagged off after tenth standard reason being distance to school at higher levels i.e. +2 schools. If they performed mediocre in their studies it was considered best to get them married by the time she did some course for stitching clothes or helped their mother's with the household chores.

In the Table 3.9, 48 per cent of the women say that mostly it was their decision to produce a number of offspring, whereas 24 per cent feel that it is entirely their husbands or elder people at home who decide. But there is very important category of 28 per cent who agreed to the fact that it was their mutual decision. These relations are quite contrary to the number of studies (Batliwala, 1999; Mukhopathgay etc.), which say that women have no control over the size of the family they are going to have and that they do not have access to birth control methods. The consequent of this next question was asked to rural women about using contraception.

Table 3.9
Decisions for Number of Children to be Produced

Women's Own Decision		*Husbands and other Elders*		*Decision Both*	
No	*%*	*%*	*No*	*No*	*%*
96	48%	48	24%	56	28%

In the Table 3.10 reflects that 79.5 per cent adopt the methods of family planning in the Shimla (Rural) 18 per cent of them responded that their husbands took care of it, whereas 2.5 per cent admitted to not using any of contraception at all. In the whole of HP the current contraception prevalence rate (CPR)[20] due to all modern methods was 53.8 per cent for whole of India; while discussing with the respondents it was found that most of the respondents relied on public sector services for contraception. People went to private sector services only in cased of emergencies. Some remuneration was given to women at the time of sterilization was also a good motivational factor. But from the overall it seemed that women were more interested and opted for contraception more readily. Most of the times the son preference was not only the pressure from family members but women themselves performed many pujas, kept fasts, and visited local devtas, so that she was blessed with a son. The proportion of knowing about male and female sterilization was 100 per cent in HP to just 48 per cent in Maghalaya.[21]

Table–3.10
The Practices of Family Planning

Who practices family planning	*Wife*		*Husband*		*None*	
	No	*%*	*No*	*%*	*No*	*%*
	159	79.5	36	18	5	2.5

Contraceptive prevalence varies from 20 per cent in Meghalaya to 67-68 per cent in Punjab and Himachal Pradesh.[22] 8 per cent of currently married women are not using contraception although they do not want any more children. These women are described as having 'unmet needs' for family planning. It these unmet needs are taken care of by more rigorous campaign of family planning the fertility rate could decline even further more. In NFHS-2, of 30,167 sterilization reported, 95 per cent are female sterilization, 79 per cent of sterilization took place before when the wife was 30.76 per cent of them obtained their contraceptives from public sector. In Himachal Pradesh also 97.8 per cent[23] of the total females sterilization was done in by public sector services.

The results from the above discussion suggests that the Government should continue to strive for maternal and child health services, it will not only improve child and maternal health but it will be act as encouragement to use contraception and lower fertility. Since son preference is also a major issue, the fertility rate is certainly greatly affected by it.

To that State instead of implementing two-child norm rigorously, it must determine and propagate policies, which enhances the status of women and transform attitudes towards the girl child.

REFERENCES

1. Ramanathan, Malathi, Women and Empowerment', EPW, April 24, pp. 1689-1697.
2. Chatterjee, J. (1985): 'The Women's Decade, 1975-85', Banhi Series, IWO, ISPCK, Delhi.

3. National Policy for the Empowerment of Women (2001), *Department of Women and Child Development,* Ministry of Human Resource Development, Government of India.
4. Sompur, Shobna and Ravi Kapur (2000), Conventional Indicators of Gender Non-Disparities Under Structure Reforms Down loaded from Internet.
5. *National Family Health Survey-2,* All India, 1998-99.
6. United Nation Economic and Social Commission for Asia and the Pacific (1999) 55th Session, Bangkok.
7. *Idem.*
8. Census of India (2001), *Distribution of Workers by Category of Workers,* w.w.w. censusindia.net.in
9. *Census of India,* 2001.
10. HPDR (2005), *op. cit.,* p. 103.
11. Mutharyappa, R., Minja Kim Choe, Fred Arnold, and T.K. Roy (1997), *Effect of Son Preference on Fertility in India,* NFHS Subject Report No. 3 NFHS, Bulletin No. 4.
12. Richmond, Julius (2000), *Excess Female Mortality in India: The Case of Himachal Pradesh,* American Journal of Public Health, September, 2000, Vol. 90, No. 9.
13. *Combined Data used from Census of India,* Net and HPDR, 2005.
14. *National Family Health Survey* (1992-93 and 1998-99), India.
15. *HPDR,* 2005, p. 46.
16. Malhi Prabhjot Gayatri Raina, Dalip Malhotra and Jagat Jarath (1999), *Preferences for the Sex of Children and its Implications for Reproductive Behaviour in Urban Himachal Pradesh,* The Journal of Family Welfare, 45(I), April, pp. 23-30.
17. *NFHS,* 1998-99.
18. *Sixth All India Education Survey,* 1999.
19. *Directorate of Education,* HP, 1999-2000.
20. *HPDR,* 2005, p. 99.
21. *NFHS,* 1998-99.
22. *Idem.*
23. *Idem.*

4

Political Empowerment of Rural Women

This chapter aims to highlight women's participation in the democratic process, their extent of awareness about the various ideologies of the political parties, and how political participation will and can translate into their welfare. If women collectively activate and represent their interests politically, it will lead to sustainability of all the other approaches. It is only through political participation their individual struggles can be brought on a common platforms, it is only through this process they will realise that their daily interactions with the environment survival needs to the addressed at the policy level.

There is persistent belief that inclusion of women into the political process or governance would change the way in which the politics of development is carried out. Woman are supposed to be concerned about the common good and that their style of development would be less corrupt and more cooperative. A macro picture based on case studies suggests that a well-established "features of institutionalized corruption makes it also rather unrealistic to expect women to be more clean politician than men (Hust, 2004:199) Women's participation in the political process will definitely increase her influence and presence in the present power definition. It will not only make the present power structure more inclusive but also women will be able to bring about changes in their legal status, direction of material and non-material resources and just to be there in some position of power to be able to influence decisions which shape her life. So that State instead of implementing two- child norm rigorously, it must determine and propagate policies which enhance the status of women and transform attitudes towards the girl child.

Until women are represented more fully in local, national, and international decision-making bodies, their issues and priorities will not receive needed resources, women fill less than 15 per cent of seats in national parliaments. Only 2.2 per cent and 5.5 per cent of the total number of members of the Board of Governors at International Montery Fund and World Bank are women. "Deep institutional change occurs when women, indigenous people, and other disadvantaged groups are given new voice and access to political power" (UN World Development Report, 9).

Yet deeply entrenched barriers continue to exclude women from meaningful participation in the political area where the decisions are made about how public resources are allocated.[1]

Moreover, the understanding of political power must be broadened to include, as Batliwala (1994)[2] puts it, the access to basic needs and services, freedom and ability to *(a)* make decisions about their own life options, for example, marry or not to marry, when where and how much to study/work where to live, etc, *(b)* make others implement one's decisions, and *(c)* to influence decisions about others in the household, community, nation and international arena at large.

Where women are excluded from general political institutions, they are not likely to have much power in community management of resources. Fighting for women's role in management requires a simultaneous all-around fight for local political power and, at the cultural level, for community recognition of women's capacities.[3] After the 73rd Constitutional Amendment Act in 1993, for restructuring local panchayats, the act mandated one-third representation to women at the village, block and district level as well as in urban municipalities. It resulted in bringing over participation albeit initially it was enforced due to traditional, cultural and social reasons, and sometimes totally due to lack of experience of public life.

There are several areas of political participation in rural areas; the first question of the series was to check whether they knew of the existing political parties.

Table–4.1
Knowledge about Political Parties

Are you aware of any names of the political parties?	*Yes*		*No*	
	No	*%*	*No*	*%*
	172	86%	28	14%

If yes, then please specify		*Congress*		*BJP*		*CPI (M)*	*Janta Dal/ HVC*
No	*%*	*No*	*%*	*No*	*%*	*No*	*%*
142	71%	134	67%	14	7%	3	1.5%

The women respondents seem to be aware about two major political parties in the area that is the Congress Party and Bhartiya Janta Party. There were only 7 per cent of the respondents who were aware of the existence of CPI (M), where as only 1.5 per cent knew of Janta Dal and regional party namely Himachal Vikas Party.

If political participation of women is studied since independence, it can safely be said that they did play a major role in the freedom movement but due to reasons unknown representation could not be continued later on. Their participation in nation building at the policy level seems to be missing. Representation of women in the state legislatures and the Parliament is low. At present women comprise 5.9 per cent of Lok Sabha members. In the 1999 elections a mere 6.5 per cent of candidates were women. Although, women consistently and persistently have lobbied for the passing of 81st Amendment Bill which proposes the reservation of one-third of the seats in the Lok Sabha. But all the political parties have discouraged repeated attempts to have the bill passed; assuming possibility that 1/3rd of them would not be visible in the parliament. In spite of such attitude, a revolution has silently taken place at the grassroots democracy through reservation for women in local government elections. Nearly a million women have entered the panchayats and local government bodies, thanks to one-third reservation in these local bodies through the 73rd and 74th Amendment of the Constitution. It is only because of this Amendment that one million women have come out of their homes and are gradually learning to use this opportunity to common advantage.

Women were further asked to elaborate on their knowledge of these particular parties, whether they found any particular difference in their functioning. Most of the women believed that they did not work for public welfare but for the people who were close to the power. Though they believed that they were all same and when it came to issues regarding women in rural areas, nobody seemed interested. They did accept the fact that with women's representation in panchayats has enabled women with traditional roles to have a voice in decision-making.

Table–4.2
Exercise of Franchise

	Yes		*No*	
	No	*%*	*No*	*%*
Have you ever exercised your right to vote?	186	93 %	14	7%
Has anybody come to you asking for Votes?	189	94.5%	11	5.5%

Most of the respondents i.e. 93 per cent accepted that they exercised their franchise. Though 94.5 per cent also added that people had come to them they reported asking for votes, no campaigns for voter awareness. Women across class, caste barriers felt that they were not accorded opportunities to participate in decision-making processes at any level and were more or less confined within strict boundaries with defined functions to perform. How important is their right to vote could not be brought into a matter of debate when the researcher discussed with the rural women. The effort to bring politics and its relation to foster change in their lives was stifled by their lack of interest and knowledge. Though they were very firm that gender justice be realized but how or if political participation could take forward this process rapidly was responded with some curious glances. It was felt that they had this innate desire to be heard and listened to on a regular and continuing basis. Their participation in the democratic process just once in five years seemed insufficient for them to partake actively in issues which influenced their lives on daily basis. They added that to bring about all round development in the villages, problems such as water and roads were still primary concerns. When the researcher and her team had gone to a peripheral village of Shimla town named Shurala, the village though in the immediate periphery of town was so badly connected that seldom any public or private transport dreads to ply his vehicle. The road reported was katcha and broken that after about covering a distance of 3 kms we had to walk down the village.

When the team walked down through the steep and narrow paths, it was difficult to fathom how the women negotiated these terrains with fodder, fuel and sometimes crops on their heads. Even after more than six decades of independence, they were still struggling and waiting for basic amenities such as roads and water.

Table 4.3
Influence on Voting Behaviour

How do you decide whom to vote for?	*To whomever husband says*		*By my own thinking*		*Influenced by others*	
	No.	*%*	*No.*	*%*	*No.*	*%*
	19	9.5%	161	80.5%	20	10%

In the Table 4.3 most of the women i.e. 80.5 per cent asserted that they decided on their own to whom to vote for 9.5 per cent voted for whomever their husband said to and about 10 per cent reported to be influenced by others' opinion. However, the second choice is also greatly influenced by the immediate environment and here also it may be other family members or spouse.

Participation has been long acknowledged as a central theme of democratic governance, where the citizens enjoy the right to participate in governance. In a political structure where freedom and equality are granted to the people, citizens can engage in political activities, at least to the extent of voting in elections and even further, they have the option to participate in a political party organization. Political participation therefore, may be defined as "those activities of citizens that attempt to influence the structure of government, the selection of government authorities or the policies of the government." (Conway, 2000)[4] It may be further illustrated that the respondents were not very sure that they could actually influence the democratic process by merely voting in a particular party. The voting behaviour in this area seemed to be more of a habit than a matter of choice.

In the Table 4.4 given above 64.5 per cent of the women respondents felt that there has been some impact on the lives of rural women due to the various policies and programmes of women. Only about 14.5 per cent felt that there has been no change in the condition of women at large. The responses of rural women necessarily depend upon their level of awareness and their understanding of the well-being of women as a concept.

Table-4.4
Change in the Lives of Rural Women due to Government Efforts

Do you think that there have been some changes in the lives of rural women due to government efforts?	*To quite an extent*		*To some extent*		*Not at all*	
	No.	*%*	*No.*	*%*	*No.*	*%*
	42	21%	129	64.5%	29	14.5%

They were further asked to elaborate what programmes and welfare activities have actually reached them. The responses were numerous and varied which are described as follows. They felt that there has been general improvement in the condition of the poor. They got certain items of ration on subsidized rates at the depot, so they were able to divert their resources to look after other needs i.e., getting a gas connection or cylinder, better health care for their family etc. The Governments efforts at providing free education are applauded almost by everyone, Balika Samridhi Yojana had also believed to help the girls in reducing the dropout rate from schools. Some respondents felt that due to the making of Self-Help Groups, women had started getting together and saving some money. This platform or the SHG meetings were also helpful in discussing various social problems confronting women. Women after having saved certain amount wanted to become independent by associating their activity with earning some income, though they mentioned that the opportunities for it were extremely limited. Indira Awas Yojana had helped certain poor people to construct a single room *pucca* house but they said it was not sufficient since they wanted employment and steady flow of income.

It is clear from the above discussion that women have not directly been benefited from the policies of the government but the area of employment of rural women needs attention by the Government in Himachal Pradesh.

To make use of the present welfare activities carried on by the government are fairly inhibited not only by their lack of information but also because of the rigid structures of patriarchy. The notions of male honour as the provider and female shame often orchestrate the women's access to public structures, blocking their access to basic amenities such as health facilities, education and employment, but also to the political process. Her lack of interest in political information further curtails her access to power.

To look at the other side of the coin, the presence of women and gender issues in parliament and policy-making is marginal, women are recognized as vote banks and politicians, both male and female, increasingly address issues of concern to women during election campaigns only as debated by Shaheed (1999).[5] She says the attention to women's issues rarely survives beyond the electoral campaigns. However, commitment to women's rights is especially fragile, inevitably the first to be sacrificed in any political negotiations and maneuvering that takes place during or after the elections.

Table–4.5
Frequency of Gram Sabha Meetings

Are you aware how frequently are Gram Sabha meetings held in your Panchayat?	*Once a month*		*Once in two months*		*Once in three months*		*Once in four months*		*Once in six month*		*Don't know*	
	No	*%*	*No*	*%*	*No*	*%*	*No*	*%*	*No*	*%*	*No*	*%*
	100	50	34	17	4	2	12	6	2	1	48	24

This question whether the women respondents were aware of the frequency of meetings held in Gram Sabha was just to quiz them to know whether they were at all interested in it or not. Though most of them said that they did not go to the meetings held due to their daily routines and they generally believed that it was sheer wastage of time since these bodies were not very effective. There were about 24 per cent of respondents who did not have any answer to the query. It may be mentioned that women have extensive workloads with dual responsibility for farm and household production. Whereas it may also be added that their work is getting harder and more time consuming due to the ecological degradation. For example, they have to go to longer distances to fetch water in times of shortage. Since there are high degrees of variations in gender roles in agriculture, environment and rural production, the most important body Gram Sabha at the rural local level must emerge as a gender sensitive to support local developmental effort.

Table–4.6
Awareness About Certain Social Evils

Do you think following social evils are present in the society?	*Dowry*		*Female foeticide*		*Domestic violence*		*Lack property rights to women*	
	No	*%*	*No*	*%*	*No*	*%*	*No*	*%*
	123	61.5	171	85.5	109	54.5	71	35.5

Table–4.7
Having an Independent View about Them

Have you ever talked about these issues and have an independent thinking about them?	*Yes*		*No*		*No opinion*	
	No	*%*	*No*	*%*	*No*	*%*
	94	47	35	17.5	71	35.5

The respondents were further asked whether they believed that certain social evils like dowry, female foeticide domestic violence and lack of giving property rights to women existed in the society. Of the total 85.5 per cent accepted that menace such as female foeticide existed in the society. They also accepted that it is more prevalent in the young couples as they wanted small families and also there is pressure of having atleast one son. Some of the women who were in the older age group argued that about 20-25 years back son preference was there in the society but they were not so much against a girl child as to kill her.

Today, they felt due to decline in social values and increased interest in materialistic lifestyle have forced young couples to opt out of girl child. What are the social, economic, psychological, health and legal issues related to it is a pointer to further research in this area.

Dowry women reported existed in the rural society but to a limited extent. They added that it was rarely demanded but these days' girls wanted to be given dowry as it enhanced their status in their in-laws house. They also felt that it was one way of sharing the property of their parents. Though most of them were not in favour of giving landed property to the daughters. Domestic violence as an evil was reported by 54.4 per cent of the respondents. Women also shared that most of the cases of minor skirmishes and beating went unreported as sometimes men considered it as exercising their right over their wife.

Crime against women is a manifestation of social insecurity and of the real lower status of women in the society.[6] "The general low status of women in the region and the entrenched nature of discriminating structures have led to what is seen as lifecycle of Violence Against Women" (VAW). Even before birth women suffer from sex selective abortion, at infancy they may face female infanticide, as young children they will have to put up with incest and son preference as adolescents they may be sexually abused or trafficked, as young women they may suffer rape, sexual harassment acid attacks; as wives they may experience domestic violence, dowry related violence, martial rape or honour killings and as widows they may be required to self-immolate or be deprived of property or dignity.[7] It definitely requires knowledge at the very local level what consists of violence; any indignity to women would be a form of violence. Himachal Pradesh falls in the category of higher-ranking rates in crime against women. Kangra, Mandi, Shimla districts have recorded high rates of crime against women. The prevalence of drug abuse among male, female headed households , migrant populations are some of the reasons for this state of affairs. Crime against women in the Himachal Pradesh[8] is only next to Madhya Pradesh and Rajasthan. To reduce the rate of crime VAW, Nyaya Panchayats should be encouraged at the rural local level so that certain issues, which get buried in households due to negligence or ignorance, get a platform to be addressed at the very local level in villages.

It can be summed up best as, Quoting UNIFEM (www.unifem.org) the target strategy paper (TSP) status;

Extending the idea of human development to encompass women's empowerment and gender justice puts social transformation at the centre of the agenda for human development and progress of women. Choices for women, especially for poor women, cannot be enlarged without a change in relations between women and men as well as in the ideologies and institutions that pressure and reproduce gender inequality. This does not mean reversing positions so that men become subordinate and women dominant. Rather, it means negotiating new kinds of relationship that are not based on power over others but on mutual development of creative human energy.... it also means negotiating new norms and rules that support egalitarian and just relations between women and men.

The words are very well said but how to put them into practice where they are most needed, how to sensitize the family and public institution which are constantly inhibiting the normal existence of women. Another question was put forward to women regarding the awareness about their rights and who was instrumental in bringing about the knowledge of it.

The rhetoric between theory and practice seemed to be the widest. About 13.5 per cent admitted to being made aware about their rights as a person by NGOs whereas in this area government agencies failed miserably.

Table–4.8
Awareness about Women's Rights

Who was instrumental in making you aware about your rights?	*NGOs*		*Govt. Agencies*	
	No	*%*	*No*	*%*
	27	3.5 %	7	3.5%

The 73rd and 74th Amendment to the Constitution has provided women with transformative opportunity. However, if the full potential of this radical beginning is to be realized, many more supportive interventions need to be put into place by the government to enhance its general achievement. Another can easily erode the advantages gained by one policy development, until and unless effective social action keeps the pressure and helps retain public spaces won by women. To quote Dereze and Sen[9] again, the low involvement of women in local representative institutions such as village panchayats is a clear illustration of this problem. In large parts of the country, local governance is in the hands of upper-caste men from the privileged classes, who are only weekly accountable to the community and often end up using local public services as instruments of patronage............. The formation of all women panchayats in parts of rural Maharashtra (Omvedt, 1990) is another interesting example of transformation of village politics based on a combination of legislative reform and political organization.

There was another issue of two-child norm an anomaly that hindered women's effective participation and leadership in local governance. This kind of qualification was adversely effecting women representation in several ways as reported by Parsai.[10] Himachal Pradesh rescinded a provision on the two-child norm in its Panchayat Raj Act and decisively moved away from the coercive approach to family welfare setting an example for others. Such a restrictive norm put women at a disadvantage forcing them to either stay out of the elections process or go in for unsafe abortion. It is not a secret that there is prevalence of son preference in the state; such norm encourages female foeticide. Invariably, the brunt had to be borne; by women either by going in for abortion or by delivering the third child surreptitiously or by being disowned by husband who would want to further his career.

There are many issues, which need to be addressed from a gendered perspective. It is a well-known fact that no society or state is gender-neutral. In order to be aware of one's rights and access them, women will have to find ways of influencing the various processes, which affect their personal and collective lives. Women have to intervene at the local, national and international areas to excess and exercise state power in order to institutionalize structural and sustainable development.

REFERENCES

1. Kelkar, Govind, Development Effectiveness Through Gender Mainstreaming , *EPW*, October 29 , 2005, pp. 46-97.
2. Batliwala Srilatha (1994): *Women's Empowerment in South Asia: Corrupt Practices*, in Change, 1-2.
3. Omvedt, Gail, 2005, *Women in Governance in South Asia*, EPW, October 29, 2005, p. 4748.
4. Conway, M.M. (2000), *Political Participation in the United States*, Third ed. CQ Press, Washington in Pratyusnna Patnaik, Affirmative Action and Representation of Weaker Sections 2005 EPW, Oct. 29, p. 4755.
5. Shaheed Farida (1999), *Politics and Power – A Gendered Perspective from South Asia*, p. 16 on Internet.
6. *HPDR*, 2005, *op.cit.*, p. 199.
7. Coomaraswamy Radhia (2005), *Human Security and Gender Violence*, EPW, Oct. 29, p. 4730.
8. *HPDR*, 2005, *op.cit.*, p. 199.
9. Dereze, Jean and Amartya Sen (1998), *Economic Development and Social Opportunity*, Oxford India Paperbacks, pp. 107-08.
10. Parsai, Gargi (2005), *Himachal Shows the Way*, *The Hindu*, 4th May, 2005.

5

Role of NGOs and Government Agency *vis-a-vis:* Women Empowerment

It is important to recognize the significance of gender issues, not in isolation but in a complete perspective of sustainable development in this mountain region of Himachal Pradesh. The problems of unemployment, inequality, and absolute poverty need growth-oriented strategies. Earlier macro level efforts by the Indian planning to address these specific problems have led to marginalisation of women and drastic marginalisation of poor women. The fact needs no reiteration that development is still considered as a bureaucratic exercise. People generally are not active participants in the process of development but are mere recipients of taking benefit through government programmes. Therefore, devolving power to the local government institutions through constitutional provisions may not ensure increased participation of women in the development process.

The rural women are often deprived of access to information, knowledge, skills and find it increasingly difficult to participate in the development activities. Women in the rural setting are less vocal and extremely occupied with household chores and agriculture activities; remain prone to manipulations by the existing local power structure. Women need not only to be active participants in planning and implementation of the programmes but also issues related to their rights, proper education adequacy of health facilities, legal literacy etc. The hiatus between people here women and government has led to the growth of catalytic agents who can foster these capabilities through closer interaction with women and work towards their empowerment where initiatives of the state have failed to do so. The role of Non-Government Organizations (NGOs) in women empowerment especially in rural areas becomes increasingly indispensable.

NGOs including women's groups have been active for quite some time to create an enabling environment for women's participation of marginalised rural women, who may be poor or belonging to lower castes. There are about 44 active NGOs in Himachal Pradesh working on gender issues centered around the problems of alcoholism, participation in self-help groups and mahila mandals, issues related to female foeticide, health, education etc. The role of NGOs has been a very important factor in providing catalytic support for the emergence of aware women by creating an enabling environment, giving training, holding workshops and mobilizing women for movements against various social evils.

Table–5.1

Knowledge of any Working NGOs in their Area

Are you aware of any NGO working in your area?	*Yes*		*No*	
	No	*%*	*No*	*%*
	143	71.5	57	28.5

Table–5.2

If Yes, please tell their names	*HGVS*		*Janwadi Mahila Samiti*		*Jan Kalyan Samiti*	
	No	*%*	*No*	*%*	*No*	*%*
	73	36.5	13	6.5	6	3

In Shimla (Rural), it was found that Himachal Gyan Vigyan Samiti (HGVS) had reached people to an extent, to act as a link between government and people between various issues and people. Voluntary organization can play a vital role in facilitating development programmes and spreading awareness. They can act as real vehicle of participation and mobilization of public, which ultimately helps in better implementation of government developments policies. They not only provide relevant information to the people but also to central state and regional agencies about the prevailing local environment. In the present system, the government's delivery system cannot be effective without cooperation and active participation of the local people.

Table-5.3
Contribution to the Welfare of Rural Society

Do you think NGOs are working for the betterment of the society?	*Yes*		*No*	
	No	%	*No*	%
	153	76.5	47	23.5

The respondents felt that these NGOs are working for the welfare of the people in general and poor in particular though the reach to the people still seemed limited considering the fact that the area of study is in the periphery of Shimla town and is better connected than rest of the rural areas which are far of from Shimla capital.

One of the important tasks that could be performed by the NGOs seemed mobilizing the local resources, which could make the government plans more realistic. Because of the informal and continuous interaction with the local people they can influence the administration and update them about the local conditions. The women most often are not in a position to safeguard their interest or take a strong step unless they are aware of their own position and believe in their ability to change the environment. If we take an example of domestic violence alone woman in a household setting may not be in a situation to say anything against it, but through organising herself she could stand up for her rights against any kind of abuse.

Table–5.4
Influence of NGOS on Women's Behaviour

Do you think because of these NGOs there have been changes in the behaviour and thinking of women?	*To a great Extent*		*To some Extent*		*Not at all*	
	No	*%*	*No*	*%*	*No*	*%*
	59	29.5	117	58.5	89	44.5

Table–5.5
Contribution of NGO's Work

Do you feel that they should continue working in villages?	*Yes*		*No*	
	No	*%*	*No*	*%*
	189	94.5	11	5.5

In the Table 5.4, the respondents about 58.5 per cent accepted that NGOs had a great influence on the behaviour of rural women. They also felt that getting together in mahila mandals, SHG meeting joined by representatives of NGOs was very enlightening since it was the only way of exposing them to various issues. They also added that things like education, health, domestic violence were non-issue to them very recently but after hearing and discussing the views of NGOs etc. they atleast now have an opinion and wish to take a stand on them. The issues which were lying buried they thought were at least brought to a platform and talked about. It was due to interventions of NGOs and group strategy that has resulted in cultivating the habit among women for saving and borrowing in the groups.

Whereas SHGs have been able to present a case for collective bargaining, the accumulated capital they feel should be utilized for Income Generating Activities. The flexibility of taking loans and meeting the credit needs of rural women have strengthened and supported their expenditure over family health, education, housing and other unforeseen expenses. The group approach of SHGs have initiated a process to be independent economically, it has given some access to capital even though very small.

In the Table 5.5, 94.5 per cent women respondents asserted that they NGOs should continue working in villages along with local people. The NGOs with their comparative advantages in reaching poor and marginalised sections of society, seeking people's participation in planning, implementation of programmes and effective ways of working with Government agencies gives them a chance to be effective collaborators. The NGOs intervention at the very grassroot level is a must for participatory overall development.

Table–5.6
Working with Women

Do you think these NGOs are working with rural women?	*Yes*		*No*	
	No	%	*No*	%
	165	82.5	35	17.5

Table–5.7
Overall Empowerment of Women by NGOs

Do you believe that NGOs are working for overall development and empowerment of women?	*Yes*		*No*	
	No	%	*No*	%
	165	82.5	35	17.5

In the Table 5.6, 82.5 per cent of the respondents admit that the NGOs work with women. It's only after forming the groups of women the NGOs make them participate in various activities, this group strategy has paved the way for rural poor women to access institutional credit but also information regarding government programmes which was earlier unthinkable for them. The NGOs have become an important like between the women and government institutions. The NGOs have been attempting to empower women through group approach.

Bezboruoh[1] reports that in HP 59 per cent of the women studied were areas of the basic issue or reservation in PRIs that was made possible due to awareness brought about by NGOs. The level of political participation was reported highest 96 per cent in H.P. The reservation has thus provided an opportunity to millions of women and avail them selves of the political space created by this legislation.

Table–5.8
Work of NGOs

Do you feel that the work of NGOs is better than government agencies?	*Yes*		*No*	
	No	%	*No*	%
	127	63.5	73	36.5

Table–5.9
Working Together NGOs and GOs

Do you think that NGOs and GOs should work together for better result?	*Yes*		*No*		*No opinion*	
	No	%	*No*	%	*No*	%
	104	52	43	21.5	53	26.5

Table–5.10
Accountability of NGOs

Should NGOs be accountable to the people?	*Yes*		*No*		*No opinion*	
	No	%	*No*	%	*No*	%
	71	35.5	51	25.5	78	39

In the Table 5.8, 63.5 per cent respondents feel that the work of NGOs was certainly better than the government agencies. The role of NGOs in the issues related to women empowerment becomes increasingly imperative just for the reason that rural women are highly segregated part of the society. The NGOs in Himachal have been actively involved in the development process and many of them are working on different issues parallel with the government agencies.

It is also an accepted fact that the NGOs style of working is not always compatible with that of the government. The relation between that of the NGOs and the government may not be very good. But the NGOs just because of their reach to the people effectively have made themselves indispensable. There is an encouraging trend to involve NGOs even at the planning level, earlier their involvement was confined only to the implementation stage. The governments however remain very apprehensive of the outcomes of involving NGOs because what they might preach may go against the prevailing ideology of the party or the local power structure.

The rural women were asked some questions regarding functioning of government agencies. Since rural development covers divergent socio-economic issues and has multi-dimensional character, it requires an administrative structure that has a feel of ground situations.

The second more important factor for implementing rural development programmes is the incorporation of community in the programmes. If the programmes involve women, the emphasis should be put on effectiveness of women participation. Garnering participation helps in mobilizing local resources but also acclimatises the programmes according to the local conditions. If the programmes have to be implemented effectively, the administration must have the capacity to translate the objectives into reality, at the same level it should be able to foresee problems and opportunities that are going to effect the implementation and identify solutions to excute the programmes.

In the Table 5.11, 1.5 per cent of the respondents were of the view that the government had worked for ameliorating the lot of women in rural also to a great extent. Whereas 51.5 per cent of women respondents felt that there has been change in the condition women to some extent

Table 5.11
Whether Government has Worked for Welfare of Women

Do you think that the government has worked for the welfare of women in rural areas?	*To a great extent*		*To Some extent*		*Not at all*	
	No	*%*	*No*	*%*	*No*	*%*
	3	1.5	103	51.5	94	47

only. It has also been seen in this study and numerous others that disparities between men and women in access to and even control of resources are closely follow-up of the women's lack of access to community governance, education, health and inadequate say in economic decision-making. It may also be added that a woman in a household may be poorer than the general economic health of the household. In this study it was felt that there was general lower status of women throughout this rural area in spite of the fact that she was putting in more hours of work than men were.

Women[2] also face social constraints such as their cultural exclusion from public spaces and activities. Public expressions of women's interest generally revolved around issues such as health-care, child-care, nutrition, domestic work, and therefore offered a socially acceptable profile of women's activities. Women's are also excluded from the mapping of natural recourse and the methods used in PRA (Participatory Rural Appraised) failed to incorporate several of the women's concern, such as these could not be expressed spatially through maps and charts.

Table–5.11
Whether the Government Efforts are Sufficient

Do you believe that the efforts made by the government are sufficient?	*Yes*		*No*	
	No	*%*	*No*	*%*
	15	7.5	185	92.5

All the respondents being from rural background and agriculture being their main profession 92.5 per cent admitted that the efforts made by the government to improve the lot of women in rural areas were insufficient since rural women were putting their labours in agriculture activities in addition to the household tasks. They wanted certain innovative ways to be introduced in making farm work easy and efficient. The women of this area also felt that they be provided with certain kind of training e.g. Silai Kendra (Stitching Centre) so that they could earn some additional income. Many of the women still complained of road, water and distance to high school.

They also felt that since the school for higher classes was at a distance, they didn't feel safe to send young girls to them. The researcher had encountered on her way back from a village, a women specially taking out time to bring her daughter from school that was 3 kms from home and forest area was on the way. They also accepted that most of the times girls after completing school in near by school were not allowed to pursue higher studies just for the reason that they could be another hand helping their mothers till they got married. Most of the respondents with whom we had long discussions never considered serious careers for their daughters though they emphasized the fact that their daughters should at least complete 10th Standard. Some women also admitted that their daughters did better in studies than their sons. Patriarchal values, well-defined gendered division of roles prompted parents to look for grooms rather pursue their daughter's career when they became young girls. However, the researcher encountered an incident in which a girl had out rightly refused to get married and wanted to pursue higher education and become a lawyer. Her resolve was so strong that after initial hostility her parents seemed to be happy with her decision.

In this study about 21.5 per cent of the respondents seemed to be aware of the government programmes. Most of the women who opted for the answer in negative were associated with self-help groups, but they also added that

Table-5.12

Awareness about Government Programmes and Schemes

Are you aware of the various income generation programmes run by Government?	*Yes*		*No*	
	No	%	*No*	%
	43	21.5	157	78.5

contributions were used for small credits and not for any income generating activities. As reported by an NGO Narantar, that 95 per cent of the total SHGs whether registered or not involved with income generating activities. It may also be added that SHGs in Mandi and Kangra are doing very well in comparison to the rest of the state. These SHGs have formed linkages amongst themselves. They sell and buy the excess produce from one SHG in a village to another. The Samridhi Mahila Cooperative in Kangra is a success story, which could be followed by other groups in the rest of the state. Women respondents had also added that they knew of the schemes like making *Haldi* (Turmeric Powder), Pickle, Jams, etc., but some how it hasn't really taken off at a big scale in this area. However, they preferred some scheme related to agriculture activity to be pursued by the Government for them, reason being that they spent most of their daily time in the fields. Lack of empowerment opportunities had emerged as major point of concern with women. They were worried not only about their employment but also of their young children for whom they felt that there were not too many opportunities.

Table-5.13

Attitude of Officials at BDO's Office and Panchayat

Are you made aware well about various type of information at the BDOs or panchayats office if you happen to go?	*Yes*		*No*		*Did not go*	
	No	%	*No*	%	*No*	%
	81	40.5	97	48.5	22	11

In the Table 5.13, it is clear that 40.5 per cent of the respondents are happy with the attitude of the officials. It is also the same group that says that they do come to know about schemes etc. but do not follow it. Whereas 48.5 per cent had complaints with the officials, they said that after going once or twice they never went to BDOs office because they never felt the need for it. Some of them also said that sometimes even after having information regarding certain schemes they do not get help. They also added that whether in Panchayats meeting or at the BDOs office, they fined themselves not able to talk about women issues freely. Though from the researcher they enquired that they wanted to make mahila mandals accommodation but had no idea how to go about it. They also wanted proper road to be made to their village but feel that they are political issues and have to be taken up politically only. It was also found that there was lack of clarity about the roles as well as relationships of the panchayats members, block and district samitis and the government departments. These were general feeling of apathy towards panchayats. Some even haplessly added nobody is bothered about them. Women in the villages felt that men went out to look for alternate jobs or daily wages. Children mostly went to school and when they come back, they want nothing to do with agriculture or looking after the cattle. They said most of the growing kids did not want to pursue agriculture as profession. It not only overburdened them with responsibilities but also got them worried about their children. This notion of abstinence from agriculture by youngsters can be attributed to two reasons, first that people do not think that agriculture is remunerative enough and second, the area under study falls in the periphery of Shimla town which raises the aspirations of young people without adequately providing for their interests. The experience of women with the government offices and panchayats seemed almost hostile, they appeared to have no expectation from the state. However, they having no replacement for the same, the government seems to formulate laws and policies aimed at correcting social and economic inequalities.

Table–5.14
Encouragement to SHGs

Are activities of self-help groups encouraged in your area?	*Yes*		*No*		*Don't know*	
	No	%	*No*	%	*No*	%
	160	80	17	8.5	23	11.5

Of the total 80 per cent of our respondents gave their responses in the affirmative about encouragement to activities self-help group most of the women had joined the SHGs recently. They were initially motivated and informed by NGOs or acquaintances. The respondents seemed to be aware of group activities their savings were reported to be low, in some groups as low as Rs. 50 month. The discussions with the women revealed that purpose of taking loans were generally i.e. expenditures on marriages, family health, repair of the house, education of children etc. This trend also indicates that women were able to cater to their needs for which otherwise they could have gone to the conventional sources for example, money-lenders or they could not have been able to look after their requirements at all. It was further revealed that borrowed money was used for consumption purposes and not utilised for any income generating activities.

Table–5.15
Benefited From SHG Activities

Do you think you have benefited from SHG activities in some way?	*Yes*		*No*	
	No	%	*No*	%
	123	61.5	77	37.5

In the Table 5.15, 61.5 per cent of the women believed that they had benefited from SHGs activities. Some of the women revealed that earlier if they needed cash, they depended generally on selling of fuel wood, fodder or a portion of their produced crops in the nearby areas. After the emergence of SHGs, they felt secure that there was something they could depend on at least in time of emergencies. They also felt that their participation in decision-making in household matters had increased after SHGs intervention.

After studying the functioning of these SHGs it is observed that these groups are functioning very well but the need to convert its activities to mainly income generation is the theme of the finding. Women were generally asked what kind of activity they would like to do specifically, the answers were not too many, to the list of making pickles, jams, stitching another was added i.e., making soft toys. This is the latest rage among young girls to learn but there is no market for it in rural areas.The adventure of the kind has to be directly associated with the needs of people in rural areas so that they do not have to go far to sell their produce. By forming linkages amongst SHGs they can cater to each other's requirements.

REFERENCES

1. Bezbouoh, Rekha (2003), *Women and Governance*, Reimagining the State, Institute of Social Sciences and IDRC.
2. Akerkar, Supriya (2001), *Gender and Participation, Bridge: Development – Gender*, Overview Report Institute of Development Studies.

6

Environment and Women Empowerment

The notion of environment assumes greater significance for the people who survive amidst and on prevailing ecological conditions. The environment necessarily entails forests, soil, water systems as well as the litany of scarcity of resources, which form an integral part of the production system such as Himachal Pradesh where most of the inhabitants work for agriculture related production. Many case studies of agrarian societies have shown that inequitable access to and control of natural resources leads to un-sustainability of environment. Since women are the prime movers of agriculture in Himachal Pradesh it is important to see the extent of awareness about the changes in environment around them. The issue of urbanization, environment degradation and its impact on their life, daily routine etc., is studied in this part of the study.

Empowering women and achieving gender equality should be a social objective as it is instrumental for the achievement of overall social and economic development. Women contribute not only to economic development but in significant ways to traditional practices regarding livelihood systems i.e. agriculture and livestock raising which is entirely subservient to ecological conditions. Under this background women empowerment and environment assumes new significance. Rural women constantly interact with the environment, however, their contribution to environment is always under played and undervalued in government policies and programmes.

To quote Sen,[1] "We need a vision of making not as patients whose interests have to be looked after, but as agents who can do effective things both individually and jointly. We also have to go beyond the role of human beings specifically as consumers or as people with needs and consider more broadly their general role as agents of change who can—given the opportunity think assess evaluate, resolve, inspire, agitate and through these means, reshape the world."

The state developments initiatives have destroyed environmental resources by over exploiting them. People and especially women, who should have been at the centre of decision-making are entirely marginalised. In fact, the erosion of biological sustainability and diversity has pauperized the land and the people. It is within this backdrop that some of the issues of a new development paradigm in rural areas are taken up.

Table 6.1
Whether Observed Change in Environment

Have you observed any change in the environment around you?	*Less fodder*		*Less water foeticide*		*Less fuel violence*		*Decrease in agriculture production*	
	No	*%*	*No*	*%*	*No*	*%*	*No*	*%*
	175	87.5	189	94.5	152	76	165	82.5

As it is evident in the Table 6.1 that most of the respondents have reported reduction in fuel, fodder, water and agriculture produce. Since these are four main pillars around which the livelihood of rural people revolve. Women's gendered responsibility of provisioning of household, their responses can be treated as first handout of the real everyday experiences. Many of the respondents said that water scarcity in summers has become a common phenomenon. The rains also have adopted an erratic pattern, they reported of excessive rains in the rainy season whereas winter season has shortened. Women's concentration in occupations like animal husbandry, traditional services, performed within a house or closeby natural environment have worsened their everyday toil and heightened the struggle for survival. An imbalance in the environmental surroundings immediately increases pressure on women to obtain pressure over women to obtain the above mentioned resources.

Consequently, increasing their work loads by way of increased time to be spent to perform each of these activities which are necessarily important for overall functioning of the family. Sometimes these particular reasons can lead to unsustainable use of natural resources in the periphery. It may also be added that increase in the number of hours spent in doing each activity reduces their chance for doing income generation activities or other self-development activity.

Rural women were further asked to give reasons what they thought could be for decrease in fuel, water and agriculture production. Majority of the women reported of cutting of trees in the name of Timber Distributions (TDs). They also felt that since the Shimla town was expanding into nearby Shimla (Rural), the land meant for agriculture purposes was sold as plots for residential colonies. Increase in population and incessant encroachment had diverted wild animals toward their residential areas. The protection of crops from monkeys had also increased their workload. Deforestation and unabated cutting of trees was sighted as major reasons for soil degradation. Division in land with in the family had decreased landholdings per household further increasing the pressure on forest area under the state. It was also reported that people used forests and natural resources indiscriminately.

Table–6.2
Effect of Urbanization on the Household

With urbanization of villages what effect has it had on your household?	*Good*		*Bad*		*Mixed bag*	
	No	%	*No*	%	*No*	%
	77	38.5	113	56.5	10	5

There were only 38.5 women respondent who felt that urbanization had brought good impact on their households. Whereas 56.5 per cent women feel that it had nothing good to offer them, 5 per cent were of the view that it was a mixed bag of blessing.

As reported in HPDR (2005), from 1971 onwards, urbanization has been constant, with the Compound Annual Growth Rate (CAGR) of urban population varying between 2.86 per cent to 3.25 per cent. During the period 1971 to 2001 the average CAGR of the urban population i.e. 9.41 per cent has been considerably higher than then CAGR of rural population i.e. 5.47 per cent. This trend is likely to increase in the future due to higher growth of population in the urban areas, which offer better employment opportunities. The consequent economic, environmental and physical changes are likely to exert pressure on the Urban Local Bodies (ULBs) to meet the growing demand for infrastructure such as land, water supply, sewerage, solid water management, housing roads etc. The sad part of the story is that urban planning takes place when towns have already pushed boundaries and entered nearby villages creating an imbalance by over using the resources meant for limited number of people.

Table–6.3
Awareness about Waste Disposal

Do you think that people in your area are well aware about waste disposal?	*Yes*		*No*	
	No	%	*No*	%
	120	60%	80	40

In the Table 6.3, more than half of the respondents believe that people in their area are well aware about ways of disposing of waste where as 40 per cent felt that they were not. It further added that villages near to towns have more problems with wastes. Certain areas in Panchayats were identified for urban waste disposal. It was due to community effort at the village level that their village was protected from becoming a dumping ground. The fact needs no reiteration that villages near the towns often have to bear burnt of being in close proximity of towns without any positive effects.

Table-6.4
Whether Urban Life is Better

If given a choice will you choose an urban life?	*Yes*		*No*	
	No	*%*	*No*	*%*
	34	17	186	83

If it is absolutely clear from the Table 6.4 that 83 per cent of the rural women responded in negative for a choice of an urban life. They further added that there is much more freedom of mobility and access to fresh environment in comparison to urban area. It was generally felt that urbanization had changed lives in villages. With urbanization people opted for modern methods to mitigate their problems for example health etc. They believed that local knowledge in regard to herbs of medicinal was fast vanishing. They said that the young generation believed in popping a tablet rather than going to forest and looking for a particular plant. Women tend to have closer interaction with the environment and natural products than men. This is probably the basic reason that women tend to possess enormous knowledge of herbs and medicinal plants and the way and means to preserve and protect them.

They are very well aware of the value and also how to preserve them. It was also found that no inventory about the medicinal, herbal or aromatic plants is available. Thus, women can be used as a latent source of information in framing strategies for preserving these plants. The future policies in this regard must ensure the needs of the people who are using the environment and natural resources on daily basis.

Table–6.5
Environment as Important Part of Life

Do you believe that environment is an important part your and your children's life?	*Yes*		*No*	
	No	*%*	*No*	*%*
	183	91.5	17	8.5

It is clear from the Table 6.5 that the respondents give due respect to the environment, 91.5 per cent of them considering it as an important part of theirs and children's life. During the course of this study it was felt that men and women are given certain social, economic and cultural roles, which also seem to influence the extent of access to control of these very natural resources. While performing various daily activities rural people come in close contact with the environment, they certainly develop their knowledge base about the area, its vegetation, extent of degradation, and also how it could be managed. The low level of awareness, literacy and education keeps them rudely away from any process of decisions-making at the local level, which might have policy implications.

Table–6.6
Whether Children have a Career in Villages

Do you think that your children after finishing their education have a career in villages?	*Yes*		*No*	
	No	*%*	*No*	*%*
	49	24.5	151	75.5

In the Table 6.6, 75.5 per cent believed that there was no career for their children in the villages. When the respondents were further asked to elaborate they clearly mentioned that there was no hope for their wards in villages if they wanted to do something else than agriculture. People in the area infact wanted that their children should opt for various other professions, but they seemed to often complain of poor standard of education in the village schools. The kids could not compete with the students who came from better or public schools. The lack of interest in agriculture was also attributed to the fact that the parents were in age group 40–50 years. That they could carry on with agriculture even if the children took no interest. As it is also evident from the previous tables that if given a choice most of the respondents wanted to remain in villages but only due to lack of infrastructure, institutions and opportunities, their children had limited options.

Table–6.7
Consideration of Women's Opinion in Policy-Making Regarding Environment

	Yes		*No*	
	No	%	*No*	%
Has your opinion ever been considered for management protection and conservation of environment policy at the local level?	43	21.5	157	78.5

There was about 21.5 per cent of the respondent who replied in affirmative that their opinion was considered at some stage in the process of policy formulation for environment at local level. However, 78.5 per cent responded in negative for the above query. It was observed that people in villages did not form unions or interacted on spatial levels about common problems. They believed in forming affiliations to the power system vertically to address their problems in isolation. This phenomenon has led to the benefit of rural development programmes to the people who were well connected with the system, whether administrative or political. The role of panchayats has further become a channel to look after the interest of well connected and not necessarily well deserved. As far as the development of a village is concerned it should be community led and women have to be an important part of the decision-making at the rural local level since institutions have to be made more participatory and inclusive.

Table–6.8
Source of Awareness about Environment Degradation

Do you think that your children after finishing their education have a career in villages?	*Yes*		*No*	
	No	*%*	*No*	*%*
	83	41.5	117	58.5

Table–6.9
Source of Awareness

If Yes, than Who?	*GOs*		*NGOs*		*Any other*	
	No	*%*	*No*	*%*	*No*	*%*
	11	5.5	71	35.5	-	-

There were about 41.5 per cent of the respondents who accepted that they had been made aware about the environment degradation whereas 58.5 per cent felt that these issues were not discussed with them at all. It was further probed that who were the sources who made them aware regarding this issues. About 35.5 per cent admitted that through NGOs they had been talking about environmental protection, consummation etc., very frequently. It was observed that government spread of awareness was limited to organizing a few seminars. These awareness programmes are still top down, do not involve people, non-transparent, hence not sustainable. Departments seem to have neither patience nor funds to promote awareness amongst people about such issues especially relevant to rural people. So, this work is often taken up by committed NGOs and such strategies in collaboration with civil society can go a long way in making people aware.

Through mode of discussion women respondents were asked whether they had any expectation from the government. Most of them were almost unanimous in their opinion that there should be more employment opportunities in the rural areas. The issue of employment is directly related to the creation of skills and scope of putting those skill into an activity through which an income is generated. A very common criticism of the rural development programmes is that they fail to cater to the needs of the more under privileged groups like women, the landless , the minorities and other deprived groups in the area. Since here we are talking only about women it requires a deeper understanding of environment, human and physical assets as source and effective delivery of basic amenities. There have been improvements in access to education, health care still remains a sector which requires lot of betterment and refinement along with other social indicators among women and children. Poor delivery of basic amentias limits progress in human development and increases pressure on environment. Women admitted to overall improvement in infrastructure but they felt that due to unemployment there was increase in migration to towns. Since the possibilities of productive employment are likely to be low in these areas migration remains the only alternative for most people.

REFERENCE

1. Sen, Amartya (2000), *Key Note Address on Tradition to Sustainability in the 21st Century at the Inter Academy Panel called Sustainability and Freedom on the International Issues,* Tokyo, May 15, 2000.

7
Conclusion and Recommendations

Conclusion

7.1 In the present study, it was found that women in rural areas spent most of their time in household chores, agriculture activities and cattle breeding. It was revealed that most of the women did not exercise their property rights. They owned landed property only after their husband died. Women respondents who were generally from younger age group had education up to Xth or XIIth standards, but did not have any vocational training or enhancement of their skills.

7.2 All of them worked up to 9 to 12 hours in a day. Their work outside home consisted of collection of fuel, fodder, water etc. They worked in fields and now an increased activity of protecting their crops from monkey menace, which had burdened their time schedules.

7.3 Most of the women did not have any property but did not mind dowry being given at the time of the marriage, since it enhanced their prestige in their in laws place and they felt that it was like taking their share of property from the parents.

7.4 Of all the decisions taken at the household level,

the decision regarding education of children was considered to be the most important whereas sharing of household work came close second. More than half of the women admitted to their opinion being taken regarding any of the household matters.

7.5 More than sixty per cent admitted to have brought dowry at the time of their marriage. They also added that dowry was never demanded but given to daughters voluntarily by parents depending on their economic condition.

7.6 A little less than half of the respondents felt that there was some pressure on them from the family to have a son.

7.7 It was women only who were adopting the methods of sterlisation and contraception

7.8 That only Congress and Bhartiya Janta Party seemed to be the most known political parties amongst rural women.

7.9 That most of the women did participate in democratic process of casting their vote.

7.10 That most of them had an interaction with NGOs regarding various issues of environment, social, economic and to an extent political.

7.11 That most of them felt that NGOs had a great influence on women's behaviour.

7.12 That most of them were part of SHGs and found that collaboration with NGOs for any collective bargaining was indispensable.

7.13 It was felt that women were not involved by the administration at the local level in implementation of either rural development programmes or for consultation for the policy formulation.

7.14 That there was penetration by NGOs in the rural areas to an extent but government agency had not been able to make headway on garnering participation of rural women.

7.15 That NGOs had changed the way women thought about certain social economic and political issues that had brought change in their behaviour.

7.16 That the group approach of SHGs have initiated a process to become independent economically, giving access to capital though very small to rural women.

7.17 That NGOs have also become an important link between the government and the rural women.

7.18 That rural women as a section of the society is highly segregated, without NGOs intervention and bringing information to the door steps of rural women, the awakening which has overtaken the connected women would not have been possible.

7.19 That rural women found the efforts of government insufficient to look after their specific needs and demands.

7.20 That administrative structure at the local level should be such that has a feel of local village level situation.

7.21 That incorporation in local community of women was ignored.

7.22 That there is lack of access to community government at the very local level.

7.23 That SHGs credit was used for consumption purposes and not for Income Generating Activities.

7.24 The activities of SHGs have increased since past couple of years.

7.25 That there was depletion of resources i.e., scarcity

of water, less of fuel wood fodder, soil degradation accompanied with increasing urbanisation. Change in climate was also reported, attributed to incessant cutting of trees.

Recommendations

The present work gives the profile of rural women in Shimla (Rural), the level of their empowerment i.e. socially, economically, politically viz.-a-viz., development and environment. The major problem, which seems to emerge, is that women though working for long hours in a day are not actually involved with any Income Generating Activities. They work as low skilled agriculture worker. Women should be provided with certain vocational training. Possibilities of livestock farming could be considerable and may provide opportunities for related activities along with handicrafts.

In coming years, the main handicap is likely to be access to water and capital investment in tubewells and small irrigation projects are likely to yield beneficial result, as land itself is unlikely to be scarce. Since these areas are not remote it may not be difficult to access services from Government and Government organizations engaged in rural development programmes. The help of teachers and health workers can be taken for training people and providing social education.

It was observed that in this area there was high preference for male child. Policy implication is that government can speed up the process by promoting the value of gender equality and by enhancing educational-vocational level, media exposure and work opportunities outside home.

The main agreement of women empowerment is that their participation must be increased at the family, local, regional, national and international spheres. The incorporation of women in governance, the exercise of decentralization be accompanied by enabling women to determine policy, so that inequality and needs of women especially poor women are accommodated within the system. This is only possible if the interests of women are reflected and safeguarded if they themselves participate in policy formulation process from the local level to international level. It also provides for the need to give funds in the hands of elected women representatives at the PRIs to be used only by them.

The rural women and young girls need to be motivated to develop interest in politics and form organizations and youth groups to address their needs. Women must also be motivated to make resource inventory of their area, which will give them knowledge of their own village and help them to have a vision to develop their constituency.

Hence, it will be useful if the Government, NGOs and training institutions engaged in strengthening local governments and helped together to take a substantial leap forward. The input of women should continue to be developed and supported and their potential further realized. There should be a visible policy of mainstreaming of women's perspective in all policies and programmes to realize sustainable development. It is evident from the study and its conclusion that the extent of women empowerment will determine the sustainability of development in rural areas of Himachal Pradesh.

Bibliography

Adeyinka Abideen Aderinto (2001): *Subordinated by Culture: Constraints of Women in Rural Yoruba Community*, Nigeria, Nardic Journal of African Studies 10 (2).

Alex Cohen, Arthur Kleinman, Bandetto Saraceno (2002): *World Mental Health Case Book*, Springer Publication.

Amartya Sen (2001): *Many Faces of Gender Inequality: An Essay*, Frontline, India's National Magazine from the Publication of the Hindu, Vol.18, Issue -22, Oct. 27- Nov. 09.

Amartya Sen (1990), *Development as Freedom*, Oxford University Press, New Delhi.

Amartya Sen (2001): *Many Faces of Gender Inequality*, Frontline, Volume 18- Issue 22, Oct-27, Nov. 09., 2001.

Amartya Sen (2000): *Key Note Address on Tradition to Sustainability in the 21st Century at the Inter Academy Panel called Sustainability and Freedom on the International Issues*, Tokyo, May 15.

Amartya Sen (2005): *India: Development and Participation*, Oxford University Press.

Andrew Dobson (1999): *Fairness and Futurity – Essays on Environmental Sustainability and Social Justice*, Oxford University Press.

Annual Administrative Report (2001-02): *Department of Agriculture*, HP.

Bina Agarwal (1986): *Cold Hearths and Barren Slopes*, London, Zed Books.

Bina Agarwal (1983): *Machnisation in Indian Agriculture: A Study Based on Punjab*, Allied Publishers Ltd. Delhi.

Barbara Harris, S. Guban and R.H. Gassen (1992) : Ed. *Poverty in India-Research and Policy*, Oxford University Press, Bombay.

C. Singh (1986): *Common Property and Common Poverty*, Oxford University Press, Delhi.

Census of India (2001): *Distribution of Workers by Category of Workers*. w.w.w. censusindia.net.in

Census of India (2001).

Claire Aster Maneja (2002): *A Thesis, Women, Weaving and the Web: An Analysis of Rural Indian Women's Agency in Attaining Economic Empowerment*, George Town University, Washington D.C.

Combined Data Used from *Census of India* 2005. Net and HPDR.

Darley Jose and N. Shanmugratnam (1999): *The Invisible Work Force: Women in the Traditional Farming System of Kerala*, Southern India, Downloaded from Internet.

Dharma Ghai (1994): Ed., *Development and Environment: Sustaining People and Nature*, Blackwell Publishers, UK.

Directorate of Education, HP, 1999-2000.

Dogra, Forest and People (1984): Published by the Author, A-Z/184, Janakpuri, Delhi.

Edward, A. Page (2002): and Michael Redcliff, *Human Security and the Environment – International Comparisons*, Edward Elgar, USA.

Farida Shaheed (1999): *Politics and Power – A Gendered Perspective from South Asia*. On Internet.

Femida Handy and Jennary Kassam (2004): *A Paper Presented at ISTR Conference*, Toronto, Canada, July.

Gail Omvedt (2005): *Women in Governance in South Asia*, EPW, October 29.

Gargi Parsai (2005): *Himachal Shows the Way*, *The Hindu*, 4th May.

Govind Kelkar (2005): *Development Effectiveness through Gender Mainstreaming*, EPW, October 29.

H. Afshar and B. Agarwal, Eds. *Women, Poverty and Ideology in Asia: Contradictory Pressures*, Uneasy Resolutions, Macmillan, London, 1989.

Himachal Pradesh Development Report (2005): *Planning Commission, Govt. of India*, Published by Academic Foundation, New Delhi.

India: Report by Govt. of India to United Nations Questionnaire on Implementation of the Beijing Platform (2005) for Action, Jan.

J. Bandhyopadhyay and Moench (1985): *India's Environment: Rises and Responses*, Natraj Publishers, Dehradun.

Jean Dreze and Amartya Sen (1998): *India-Economic Development and Social Opportunity*, Oxford University Press.

Jean Dreze and Amartya Sen (1998): *Economic Development and Social Opportunity*, Oxford India Paperbacks.

Jeffrey Sachs (2005): *The End of Poverty*, Penguin Books.

Julian Agyman, Bullard, D. Robert and Bob Evans (2003): *Just Sustainabilities – Development in an Unequal World,* Earthscan Publications.

Julius Richmond (2000): *Excess Female Mortality in India: The Case of Himachal Pradesh,* American Journal of Public Health, September, Vol. 90, No. 9.

Kartik, C. Roy, and Cal Clark (1994): *Technological change and Rural Development in Poor Countries – Neglected Issues,* Oxford university Press.

Kasturi Gupta Menon (2004): *(W &E) Attaining the MDG in India,* The Role of Publication & Service Delivery.

Kerril Davidson-Hunt, (1998): *Class, Gender and the Commons in the Indian Himalayas, in the Sustainability in Fountain Environments John Sinclair,* Fibret Berkes and James Gardner, Downloaded from Internet.

Kim Berry (2005): *Gender and Social Equity in Community Water Management, University of North Carolina at Ashenvile,* not yet a fully developed paper.

L. Gulati, *Profiles in Female Poverty,* Pergamon Press, London, 1982.

Lars Rudebech, Ed. (1997): *When Democracy Makes Sense,* ADUT, Uppala University, Sweden.

M.M. Conway (2000): *Political Participation in the United States,* Third ed. CQ Press, Washington in Pratyusnna Patnaik, Affirmative action and representation of weaker sections 2005 EPW, Oct. 29.

N.K. Bannerjee (1998): Challenging the Patriarchal Ethos of Society had never been the Agenda of the Indian State.

National Family Health Survey (1992-93 and 1998-99), India.

National Family Health Survey-2, *All India,* 1998-99.

National Policy for the Empowerment of Women (2001): *Department of Women and Child Development,* Ministry of Human Resource Development, Government of India.

National Policy for the Empowerment of Women, 2001: *India – Source' Department of Women and Child Welfare.*

P. Bardhan (1984): *Land, Labour and Rural Poverty,* Oxford University Press, New Delhi.

P.K. Rao (2000): *Sustainable Development – Economics and Policy,* Blackwell 'Publishers.

Page and Czuba, *Journal of Extension,* Oct., 199, Vol. 37, No. 5.

Paul Marc Henry (1991): Ed., *Poverty, Progress and Development,* Kegan Paul International, UNESCO.

Prabhjot Malhi, Gayatri Raina, Dalip Malhotra and Jagat Jarath (1999): *Preferences for the Sex of Children and its Implications for Re-Productive Behavior in Urban Himachal Pradesh*, The Journal of Family Welfare, 45(I), April,[1] NFHS.

R. Dixon (1978): *Rural Women at Work: Strategies for Development in South Asia*, Baltimore, Johns Hopkins University Press.

R. Mutharyappa, Minja Kim Choe, Fred Arnold, and T.K. Roy (1997): *Effect of Son Preference on Fertility in India*, NFHS subject report No. 3 NFHS Bulletin No. 4.

Radha Coomaraswamy (2005): *Human Security and Gender Violence*, EPW, Oct. 29.

Rajan Krishanmurthy, (1995): *Gender Issues in Agriculture and Rural Development Policy in Asia*, TAO, RAP Publication.

Rajni Kothari (1988): *Rethinking Development – In Search of Human Development*, Ajanta Publications.

Lakshmi Rao and Krishna Rao (2000): *Status and Advancement of Women.*

Regina Scheynens (2000): *Promoting Women's Empowerment through Involvement in Ecotourism.* Experiences form the Third World, Journal of Sustainable Tourism, Vol. 8, No. 3.

Rekha Bezboruah (2003): *Women and Governance*, Reimagining the State, Institute of Social Sciences and IDRC.

Sabine de Rooij, Institutional Capacity for Rural Women's Empowerment, *Electronic Journal of Polish Agriculture Universities*, 2005, Vol. 8, Issue- 3.

Shobna Sompur and Ravi Kapur (2004): *Conventional Indicators of Gender Non-Disparities Under Structure Reforms*, down loaded from internet.

Shruti Pandey, (2005): *Property Rights of Indian Women*, www. co.za/ Conference.

Sixth All India Education Survey, 1999.

Srilatha Batliwala (1994): *Women's Empowerment in South Asia: Corrupt and Practices*, in Exchange Change.

Srilatha Batliwala, ASPBAE (1995): *Defining Women Empowerment–A Conceptual Framework*, Fourth World Conference on Women. Beijing., Sept.

Srilatha Batliwala (1997): *What is Female Empowerment*, Paper Presented in Seminar on Female Empowerment and Demographic Process, Moving beyond Cairo, International Vision, for the Scientific Study of Population.

Stefanie Strulik (2004): *Women – Panchayat- Electives at the Interface of State and Village Politics*, Paper on the 18th European Conference on Modern South Asia Studies at Land University, Sweden.

Supriya Akerkar, (2001): *Gender and Participation, Bridge: Development-Gender*, overview report Institute of Development Studies.

Tenth Five-Year Plan (2002-07): *Planning Department*, Government of Himachal Pradesh.

The Millennium Development Goals, Report (2005): UN, New York.

U. Sharma (1980): *Women, Work and Property in India*, Janistock Publishers, London.

Uday Desai, Ed. (1998): *Ecological Policy and Politics in Developing Countries*, State University of New York Press.

UNACC (1999): *Inter Agency Committee on Women and Gender Equality.*

United Nation Economic and Social Commission for Asia and the Pacific (1999) 55th session, Bangkok.

V. Jose, Ed. (1989): *Limited Options: Women Workers in Rural India*, International Labour Organization, Asian Regional Team for Employment Promotion, New Delhi.

V. Shiva, Staying Alive (1988): *Women, Ecology and Survival*, Kai for Women, Delhi.

Vinay Tandon (2002): *Getting Women to Choose – Case Study on* Sustainable Livelihoods and Poverty Alleviation, "Mountain Forum E-Consultation for the UNEP/Bishek Global Mountain Summit.

W. Fernandes and S. Kulkarni, Eds., (1983): *Towards a New Forest Policy, People's Rights and Environmental Needs*, Indian Social Institute, Delhi.

Women's Human Rights Net Association for Women's Rights in Development (AWID).

World Bank (1987): "Environment, Growth and Development" *Development Committee, World Bank*, Washington DC.

World Bank (1988): "Environment and Development, Development Committee," *World Bank*, Washington, DC.

World Commission on Environment and Development (1987).

Index